The Newly Tattooed's Guide to Aftercare

Aliza Dube

Published in North America and Europe by Running Wild Press. Visit Running Wild Press at www.runningwildpress.com Educators, librarians, book clubs (as well as the eternally curious), go to www.runningwildpress.com for teaching tools.

ISBN (pbk) 978-1-947041-49-3
ISBN (ebook) 978-1-947041-50-9

Printed in the United States of America.

***

"You shall not make any cuts in your body for the dead nor make any tattoo marks on yourselves: I am the Lord. Do not profane your sister by making her a harlot, so that the land will not fall to harlotry and the land become full of lewdness"
- Leviticus 19:28

***

Waiver: I hereby confirm that I am not under the influence of drugs or alcohol at the time of this tattoo.

***

"You guys wanna watch?" I ask. I'm on my tiptoes looking over the counter that separates the waiting room from the actual tattoo parlour in Til Death Tattoo in the Old Port of Portland, Maine. The shop looks like the brick basement bedroom of the angsty older brother I never had. Pencil sketched pin up girls bat their eyelashes at me from the walls, pinned behind glass like butterfly specimens, beautiful and trapped. I'm a little unsteady on my feet from the shot of bravery I took in the car. Matt and Alex are flipping through a book of piercing examples. They stick on the final page a little too long. It's got a pic of a vag piercing. I roll my eyes. I expected more from my college guys.

"Sure. I wanna see you scream," Matt replies. I keep my "That's what he said" comment to myself because summer is over. This is not where me and Matt are anymore. We are bros now. Just friends. No benefits involved anymore. He's got pink hair now, ten pounds lighter now. This is not what *my* Matt looked like. He is not *my* Matt anymore. I heard a theory once that said if two ex-lovers are still friends, then they either were never in love to begin with or are in love still. I guess I'm still waiting to figure out where we stand.

Alex is my new favorite maybe and Matt's new best friend, a one night stand but I'd love to make it two. When I close my eyes, I can still see the trails my fingernails had left, like wings, on either side of his vertebrae last weekend, and the memory of this small destruction leaves me smiling. He's fiddling with a fresh septum piercing. Shoulder length hair, suspiciously skinny, and a collection of longboard scars. He talks about longboarding a lot. He says it's easy, you just have to come to terms with the fact that gravity exists, that you fall sometimes. He reminds me of enough ghosts to be my next one.

There is one chair for emotional support in the studio. Matt takes the seat, Alex takes Matt's lap. They mock pose like they're a couple. They wait expectantly, watching for me to lose my mind as the hipster tattoo artist puts the needle to skin. I don't even blink.

My hands are shaking though. The hipster is trying to steady them, trying to keep my wrist still so he can carve a pine tree into it. It catches me off guard. I'm not used to somebody holding my hand and this makes them shake more. I'm not nervous; this is just what my hands do lately. They have their own Richter scale. Even my snapchats turn up blurry. I am a Junior in college and I am anxious almost all the time.

"Have you ever gotten a tattoo before?" The tattoo artist asks, concerned that my tree is going to end up looking like a jellyfish. He's trying to be compassionate, but I'm not sure he knows how. He's got a tattoo of a hatchet over his ear and I'm pretty sure I could fit my fist through his gauged ears. Pain is a stranger to him, either that or a very close friend. His name is Steve and this is the unlikely beginning of a beautiful friendship.

"Yeah, I got two on my ribs," I say in reference to the prison quality sparrow and elephant that I had gotten at the no name shop in my hometown. Matt and Alex are swapping looks, like the tats I've mentioned are some hole in the wall only they've visited. I'm busy watching the needle's hungry mouth eat up my skin, leaving black space where the flesh my mother gave me used to be. The black is fresh, new, it's a story I am choosing to tell for myself, laid above the one that nature dealt me.

The boys grow bored with my indifference and leave in search of caffeine. That's fine. I don't need anybody to hold my hand. I've done this before and will do it again.

***

The Rules of Aftercare
1. Under No Circumstances should you leave the bandage on
for more than two hours

***

I'm in the Hannaford's lady's room, trying to peel off the shrink wrap surrounding my fresh ink. Matt and Alex are shopping for something to mix our tequila with because we don't want to die tonight. Because that's what legend tells us; only the crazy or the damned drink tequila with no chaser. We are not committed enough to fall under either category. This hospital grade tape stuck on my wrist hurts worse than the needle. Curses are flying out my mouth with the frequency of commercial flights.

"MOTHER FUCKING CHRIST!!!"

"Language!" the old lady in the handicapped stall scolds, for the fifth time.

"SON OF A FUCKING BITCH!!!"

I can only imagine what the shoppers passing the bathroom door are thinking. I honestly don't give a fuck. I'm in pain ripping off the world's worst motherfucking band-aid. The tape comes off with more arm hair than I was even aware I had. I toss it in the trash with contempt.

I run through the aisles shouting Matt and Alex's names like a lost child searching for a parent. Alex waves to me with a flask from the booze aisle. I gaze at my warped reflection in the amber faces of bottles on the shelves. I am always amazed by how many different ways there are to get drunk. The grocery store offers more varieties of alcohol than cereal or toothpaste, as if to say that what you need to escape life will always be more important than what you need to actually live it.

I cannot help but think that the three of us look like a lost Indie band in the sea of this suburban grocery store; Matt with his pink hair and pug nose, Alex with his ponytail, his septum piercing gleaming, Me, in Courtney Love black lace and ripped nylon.

"Hey, I've got one of those!" I exclaim, referring back to the flask that Alex holds in his hand, like this is the world's rarest coincidence.

"I'd expect nothing less," Alex says.

"It's got Marilyn Monroe on it," I explain. "And it says, a good girl knows her limits, but a wise girl knows she has none."

He shoots me that sideways smile he reserves for when I say

something that's a cocktail of cute and self destructive. I love that smile. I've only seen it one or two times before, but I'd do anything to make that smile happen.

"And that… is how you die," Alex condemns. And I'm ok with this, because Alex shot me that "poor baby" smile. This is the story I am choosing; I am the wise girl with no limits.

***

2. Use Antibacterial soap and water and wipe tattoo completely clean

***

We're in Matt's dorm room, back from our afternoon adventures. This is only the second time I have visited Matt at his school, 2 hours away from my own. The place still feels new, like a grown up tooth breaking through the gum line. Fresh and strange. Unstained. Matt's room is a collection of everything he knows his mother would detest. A poster displaying different strains of weed covers most of the door, that we keep locked at all times. Paranoia is something that demands privacy. A yogibo sprawls across the floor with the apathy of a beached whale. A graveyard of empty bottles are set up like bowling pins under the desk, and if the RA ever sees this, it will be Matt's last strike.

My wrist burns but smells like Velvet Sugar. I had accidentally spritzed my tattoo with Bath and Body Works spray and now my open wound smells like a Victoria's Secret fitting room. "Open wound" is the word the tattoo artist had used to explain the significance of the aftercare to me. "You're dealing with an open wound here— you've got to be careful with it until it heals." I didn't know how to explain to him that I had no patience for instructions like that. If things healed right in my world, they did so by accident.

"Spray the door," Matt instructs. D'Arretti is rolling spliffs on Matt's desk. I'm not sure what I think of this new character, who reminds me of something from Looney Tunes come to life. He's got a Salvador Dali mustache and a shock top of dyed red hair. Fifteen minutes ago he shook my hand and introduced himself as the dealer of the third floor. $5 per spliff. He'd kissed my hand like I was visiting royalty. He eyed my stilettos like they were candied. The more people I meet, the less I believe normal exists.

We've got a window cracked, but it still smells less than legal in this dorm room. I'm using the perfume my Mama mailed to me at summer camp as a cover. She'd be so proud. Matt is panicking, wringing his hands with weed-shot paranoia. D'Arretti is humming along to Spotify Premium oblivious to his distress.

"You only know you love her when you let her go…."

"This song reminds me," D'Arretti says to no one in particular, "Of a girl I once loved— still love to this day." He slows his rolling and stops to look directly at me. Under his gaze, I am self conscious of every pore, every inch of my skin. He looks at me like he's known me for a century. I shiver. "You got one of those, girly? Someone you love but would never soberly agree to being in a relationship with again?"

I want to tell this stranger that I do. That I feel this love's absence like an amputee feels a phantom limb or in the way a child's tongue searches sleepily for a lost baby tooth. I want to talk about how my head still spins toward whatever voice speaks his name, that I have a recognition for its syllables as if they were my own. My mouth opens as if to speak, but I can't bring any of the words up. Matt's new girlfriend opens the door, all heart shaped face and blonde skull. I refuse to speak about heartbreak. That would imply that I have a heart to break. This is not the story I want to tell.

***

3.Next apply a thin layer of Aquaphor. Repeat this step 3 or 4 times a day to prevent the tattoo from drying out.

***

Matt's friend, Lily, a mousy and unremarkable girl, had said that I could borrow her Aquaphor she had leftover from her own tattoo. She had also said we could borrow her blender for the margarita mix. Lily had apparently forgotten about these promises, because we are now sexiled from her room. My fresh ink is crinkling like a dying leaf. We are drinking the tequila straight out the bottle- the mix Matt bought left untouched in the fridge.

I'm sitting next to Dio and Molly on Matt's yogibo. Dio and Molly are Matt's neighbors. They are roommates and maybe something more? It's impossible to tell with this crowd. Dio has that kind of perma-tan that can make any face beautiful, as if she needed help in that department. She's an Esmeralda straight off the Disney screen with a lip stud for irony. Dio is Latin for god and she doesn't let me forget it. Molly's all boyfriend jeans and boyish figure. Matt mentioned once that she has a long distance boyfriend. We don't talk about him though. She sports a t-shirt that's a warped version of the Starbucks logo. "Dapacino" it reads. An incrimination. An identity. We all compliment her t-shirt at least once; it's a custom of our culture. The three of us are circle of deathing the first fifth of tequila like winos living under the interstate. We try to hide our winces after each sip. It looks too much like weakness.

Matt's new girlfriend looks a lot like me, all heart shaped face and blonde bleach, but I'm not drunk enough to comment on this yet. She is nestled in his lap and he kisses the nape of her neck occasionally, like he used to kiss mine. I feel like I'm having an out of body flashback to two months ago, watching them. Blood flushes to my cheeks. In jealousy? In irritation? I'm like a five-year-old sometimes, expecting that everything I lick should be claimed as mine, indefinitely. With nearly a dozen flings behind me, you'd think that I'd have learned to give up on this possessiveness. But it's a haunting I've never been able to exorcise. I'm working on trying to bury the past. I'm trying to grow something new here in the rubble.

Alex is sitting dangerously close to the open window. There's no screen and he looks as though he's deciding whether or not it would be worth it to tumble the three stories to the ground. His eyes are wide kiddie pools of Salvia, a legal hallucinogen that until this summer I had no idea existed. I'm timing out eight minutes until he's back from his trip. There is a joint tucked defiantly behind his ear. He could have easily hidden it, but he has his hair scraped back into a ponytail. He'll walk past his RA like this, challenging them to call him out on it. They never will. Is this fearless? Reckless? Or are we just stupid?

I shake my head. The boys need a light. I need some air.

***

4. When the Tattoo starts peeling…

***

The stairwell down from Matt's room smells like basement, all metallic with traces of weed from all those souls who were too impatient to make it through the front door. In the lobby, the RA on duty wrinkles his nose suspiciously at us from behind the front desk. He doesn't recognize me. I am not supposed to be his problem, but here I am, near barefoot on the tile floor. "Whose responsibility is she?" the RA demands around a mouthful of Cheetos. Alex and D'Arretti both shrug as we race out the door. This is one of the most accurate statements I have ever heard.

D'Arretti, Alex and I are in the campus courtyard, playing in the early night. It's only 9, but the stars dance like midnight. D'Arretti and Alex are smoking. I'm freezing. I'm running around on frost pricked pavement in tights so threadbare my toes poke out the front, like I'm homeless. I've abandoned my heels for the night, they can retire, they've already made their point. The boys are watching me like I've jumped out of a fairy tale, like my appearance is something they can't quite believe. I love this look they've got on their faces. I'd do anything to make this look happen.

"Did you buy those like that?" Alex asks, plucking a loose thread on my knee like a guitar string. He's got the voice of a fifty-year-old smoker, threadbare in all the right places.

"No, they're an experiment," I say. Alex shoots me that "poor baby" smile I adore. "I got these freshman year. No rips. I want to see what they look like by the time I graduate." That had been the intention, anyway, but I don't think the fabric can hold up for another year and a half. Alex and D'Arretti gawk at my knees poking through the tears.

"They're a metaphor for my soul," I think to myself. I shake the thought away. I don't repeat it aloud. The thought is not my own. It's a leftover from my Catholic childhood. A soul is a belief that my mother had given me. It's something I donated to Goodwill long ago, with my Barbies and jumpers. Outgrown. I trace my tattoo gingerly with a fingertip. The ink is swollen, it feels like braille beneath my skin. I have written over my mother's draft with my own story now. You can't even read her handwriting anymore.

***

5.No Tanning

***

I sink down on the yogibo in Matt's dorm room. I can't remember how I got here. In my mind there are brief snippets of memory, like the reel from an old silent film. There's a stairwell, the glide of tile beneath my toes. There was the groan of a door being unlocked reluctantly and in the background someone laughing. I'm pretty sure that was me.

Second hand smoke is woven through my hair like a braid as if it's a natural part of me. Dio's sitting next to me, but it takes me a second to realize because her face is busy kissing Molly's. She spins to face me, wiping Molly's lip gloss off the corner of her mouth.

"Are you bi?" She asks.

Without a beat to contemplate what border I am about to cross or what passport I will need to declare to get there, I nod my head. Her lips meet mine before I even have time to catch my breath. Katy Perry had promised me cherry chapstick, but Dio tastes like weed and tequila, just like me.

I open my eyes. Matt is staring at me, his eyes wide, startled. It's the same look he gives me when I knock a shot back like it's water or when I drink straight from the bottle. This is what I like to call his "lifeguard face." It says, baby you're drowning. Out of your depth. In over your head. But he never moves a toe from the shore. I don't need him to save me. My story has come a long way since he last left it.

***

6. No Swimming

***

I'm drowning, not in water, but in limbs, in boys' lips mapping out my anatomy as if I don't already know where everything is. I just wanted Alex, but somehow ended up with D'Aretti too, on the porch of the admissions building. Alex had wanted to longboard. I had wanted to watch, maybe try it out for myself. The longboards are now propped against the railing, abandoned along with the best of my intentions. Now I'm caught in the middle- literally, wondering how to admit that I'm only down for two-thirds of what this is shaping out to be. I've got my back to Alex. He's toying with my Led Zeppelin earring between his teeth, his hands about my waist like we're at a school dance. D'Arretti has his fingers tangled in my hair, biting my lip a little while he's kissing it. I taste blood. I dig myself closer into Alex, trying to disappear into his sweatshirt, but his wasted mind offers little sanctuary for me now.

"We shouldn't," D'Arretti pulls away. I catch my breath, relieved. But his eyes are still hungry and he still keeps talking. "Do this here. We should go inside or find a bush or something."

I'm waiting for Alex to tell D'Arretti to fuck off. To explain that I am his and his alone. Alex doesn't say anything though. I feel his chin nod up and down against the back of my head in agreement. I'm staring down at the borrowed shoes I am wearing because I can't look either of them in the eye. *Take a walk in someone else's shoes.* Maybe the owner of these loafers would be braver than me, brave enough to be honest about her limits. I am nothing but a scared little girl with someone else's tongue in my mouth.

Between the smoke of the boys' snuffed cigarettes my heart is screaming for air. Because now I know just how much they think of me. This is not the love story I was writing.

***

7. Call T'il Death for Any Further Questions

***

I rest my bones on the yogibo. I clench and unclench my fists, trying to warm the outside out of them. I don't remember climbing the staircase or walking down the hall, but I am here. If I don't think about it too hard, I can pretend that I never left at all. I got one leg on Molly's and the other on Dio's. It's a throne for a false queen. Frankie, one of Matt's friends who looks like an English teacher I had in high school, a sandy beard and thin rimmed glasses, is listening from where he sits on Matt's vacant bed. He is laughing a little too hard at everything I say.

"No I don't believe in monogamy.

If I ever have a kid it will be Chance, for a boy, and Karma, for a girl, because that's what they will be. Maybe Patience, because that's what I'll need if they turn out anything like me.

I don't believe in love. I believe in chaos— always."

I'm waiting for someone to catch the irony, for someone to notice the smirk of a lie on my lips. But no one ever does. I don't believe the things I say, it's a script I wrote long ago, a part I have to play. My tough girl facade with her shell-shocked eyes fools them. Underneath I'm still waiting for my life to become the romantic comedy my mother's movies promised me it would be. Because that's how it works, right? The cynical girl always gets the guy?

Matt is asleep in his girlfriend's room. Even though I just fucked Alex, he is nowhere to be found. I will not go looking for D'Arretti. Dio holds Molly's hair back as she spills her guts into the wastepaper basket. I feel abandoned, even though I know I am no one's responsibility but my own. I'm beginning to lose track of the plot line of my own existence. Frankie holds out his hand. I take it. I let him lead me to what he calls home, an identical dorm room box down the hall. I can barely tell the difference.

***

8. We Offer Free Touch-ups If Needed.

***

When Frankie gets bored with fucking me, he kisses me on the back of my neck. He tucks me into bed like I'm a child, turns out the light, and shuts the door. I don't think to ask him where he is going or if he will be back. His alarm clock carves red angry numbers into the night. 11:09. It's too early to be asleep on a Saturday night. I fling myself out of bed and paw around for the yoga pants I had snagged from my duffle on the way out of Matt's room. They have a pinky sized hole on the ass, but I don't care. I'm stumbling down the hallway, and the walls keep moving. The hallway's getting longer. I think of Alice trying to find the garden, her wonderland. I'm like Alice, I think. But I no longer have anything I'm looking for and the metaphor falls flat.

A door flings open and Chance the Rapper steps out. Or at least a guy who looks like him.

"Having a fun night?" he asks with a look that's usually reserved for Disney villains. He gestures to my neck. I catch a glimpse of myself in the hallway mirror. It looks like I've been choked. But I know better, it's the ghosts of five hungry mouths on my skin: *Alex, D'Arretti, Dio, Molly, Frankie.*

"I think he missed a spot," he says it like it's an oversight that must be corrected.

***

9. No Scratching

***

He's pulling me by the arm into the lady's room. He flicks the doorstop out of the way with his foot so that no one will follow us. *Please, someone, follow us,* I think but am too slow to scream. He pulls me into the shower. He stares at me as though he expects me to perform a magic trick for him. I don't move. I don't believe in magic anymore. He kisses me, toying with the hem of my tank top.

"I don't know you," I protest. My arms stay at my sides. I'm tired, so very tired. He digs around in his pocket and pulls out a Trojan as if this is all the consent he needs.

Matt and Alex's names are caught in my throat. I want to scream, want them to come rescue me because this is what happens in the movies. The girl always gets saved. But this stranger's got me pressed against the wall. A bruise is blooming under his grip on my arm. He's sealing out my voice with a kiss. My limbs are heavy, my eyelids are heavy on tequila, on apathy. I start counting floor tiles, counting seconds. I kiss back.

"He's gonna notice I'm gone," I protest. I'm vague about the "he". I don't know whether I'm talking about Frankie, Matt or Alex. Or an imaginary boyfriend. I'm trying to scare this guy off, saying hey— somebody gives a shit about me. He doesn't seem to believe me anymore than I believe myself. He doesn't even acknowledge that I spoke at all.

I pretend this is my choice as my yoga pants pool over the shower drain. I pretend it's another one of my reckless stories. I pretend it's like a G-eazy song, like this is something to cross off my bucket list. I begin writing the story I will tell my friends, the story I will tell Matt and Alex.

I mine my soul for a meaning in this because the book of my life has to make sense. I pretend I'm not about to cry.

***

10. Consult a physician at first sign of infection.

***

Frankie's door is locked. I locked myself out. I don't have a key. This is not where I live. I don't know where Frankie is or when he's coming back. I don't really want to sleep in Frankie's bed, but I don't really want to sleep in the hallway either. I cringe at the thought of another (let's face it, stranger) pressed against my skin. I want to throw up. I have never been more aware of my liver in my life.

I slump against the wall. My eyelids droop, my limbs are heavy. My fingertips trace the bruise on my arm gingerly, wondering if tomorrow I will be able to play it off as a hickey. I don't want to process what just happened. I'm wishing that life had a backspace key, that I could just delete the past hour with the click of a button. If no one ever gets the real story, then it didn't really happen, right?

I'm dozing. I'm waiting for someone to let me in. Someone to care. Someone to give me a place to call home for the night. I'm scratching at my wrist, at the day old tattoo stamped there. Has it really only been a day? The outline is red and angry, my skin rejecting the ink injected there. My body knows this doesn't belong, my immune system is trying to get rid of the pigment but it can't. This open wound is more than skin deep. I'm shaking my head at the little girl who thought she could control the story. The little girl who's still trying to, even though the plot stopped making sense a long time ago. She doesn't understand that you can't control the story, the story controls you.

How to Run Away

You spend the last week of the cross country season on the stationary bike. After visiting Matt last weekend, you have a broken toe and a hangover that never seems to go away. You tell your coach that it was a longboarding accident that put you out of commission. You were actually too drunk to recall. No, not too drunk to recall, too proud to admit, too numb to feel that your foot got slammed in the closing of a bathroom door at the hands of a stranger. You've never been on a longboard long enough to break anything. You, however, cannot say the same for the hands of strangers.

Your coach is too religious, too strict, too old. He doesn't know what to do with you, he has to wipe the relief from the corners of his crinkled paper bag mouth when he tells you to go cross train. You are no loss to him, not fast enough to matter. You are a liability he never liked much anyway.

Friday is the Halloween dance. Saturday is the state meet, a real doozy and a predicament. Coach has forbidden everyone on the team from going to the dance. You're there anyway. You could never really follow directions, you could never really say no to a good time, you could never really handle being alone.

You're wearing a dress with no back to it. It's all black lace and hot pink satin. It makes you feel some kind of Geisha girl, Miss Mary Mack with buttons all down her back. It makes other people think of escorts, think easy, think opportunity, think all the dirty words our mothers always told us not to say in public. But you've never really cared what other people think anyway.

There is a boy pressed to your back, covering what the fabric of your dress can't make up for. He is a squinty eyed, big nosed, skeletal frame brand of nope. It doesn't matter. You don't plan on going home with him anyways. You do plan on looking chosen, flirtatious, yet unavailable. You're some kind of music box dancer, spinning to her own track, knowing little else but standing on her own two feet. You pull at the front of your slip compulsively. You're constantly keeping yourself in check so as not to flash an unsuspecting and hungry audience. Rihanna's voice is booming out the speakers, talking all sticks and stones and sex. There is a ring of boys around you, all dressed like Clark Kent. You can no longer tell their faces apart. It doesn't matter anyway, you can't find Superman anywhere in their PBR and weed-stenched midst.

Your four inch heels kill. You can feel your bone cracking just a little deeper each time your foot meets the dance floor. You're feeling tequila at the back of your throat; tonight's tequila, last weekend's tequila, you are drowning in every sip you've ever taken. The nope boy reaches for your crotch with shaking fingers. It's time to leave. ASAP Rocky is rapping about having a fucking problem too loud over the speakers. You hit the ground running. You tear your shoes off like a drunken Cinderella, except there will be no trace left of you tomorrow, no fairy tale trail of breadcrumbs. By the light of day you will be MIA, not that anyone would bother to look for you anyway.

You catch dirty looks from the campus police at the door. You shrug your strapless shoulders at them on your way out of the student center into the frost pricked night. You are through with the opinions of men for the evening.

Your stilettos are slung in between your blood red fingernails. A stranger is sitting on the grass overlooking the commuter parking lot, all Carhartts and flannel, lumberjack kinda cuteness. "Who are you supposed to be?" He asks you.

He hands you a cigarette, lights it for you as if you don't know how it's done. Your ears are ringing in the sudden quiet. The music from the dance pulses in the distance, urgent and faint as a muffled scream. You shiver, you had been too brave, too arrogant to bring a jacket. You ask him, "What kind of question is that supposed to be?"

"No," he says. "what's your costume?" You stare at your stripper, second skin dress. The satin is slick with some other body's sweat. Your neckline is inching dangerously low. You will look at the stranger, a safe, tough boy with callouses on his hands, the love bites of hard work. He doesn't wear a costume either. You think about the future of this boy, a wife, a pair of kids born into wedlock, a humble house. You see only good things coming for this boy, and that's all you would ever wish for him. You only wish that you could say the same for yourself.

"I went as myself," you tell the stranger, even though you're not really sure who that is anymore.

The boy has better manners than to follow you home. When you open the door to your apartment, you are what you fear most: alone. You go to bed with the lights on. You've made this a habit ever since the "incident". A friend that you've confided in tells you this is reasonable. You think there is no reason a twenty-year-old woman has to sleep with a night light. She tells you to go talk to someone if you are scared, if you are upset, if you are hurt. You are afraid of everything. You never stop being angry at yourself. Some days it hurts to breathe. You tell no one. It's nobody's business but your own and the electric company's.

You will board the Cross Country bus at 7 am with the rest of your team. You will be armed with a baja sweatshirt, a can of Monster Rehab and an oversized pair of sunglasses. You will not bother to pack your sneakers. The Halloween sun will drill at your temples. You question the gods you worship in these pursuits, but, in the end, this is all you know. You will never run a Cross Country race again. You will tell yourself this suits you. You will tell yourself you're on to better things.

The following Monday, coach calls you into his office, a basement closet with his name in gold plating on the door. The office smells like old socks and icy hot. There is only one window, about the size of a shoe box, crosshatched over with tiny chainlinks. It makes you think of prison in all the wrong ways.

He will ask you why you disobeyed. You will tell him it was because you wanted to. You will not give him the apology he is fishing for. His old man mouth will droop open like a fish out of water, confused and betrayed. Angry. He never did know what to do with you, he doesn't know what to do with you now. He will ask the captains, your roommates, how to punish you next season. There will be no more Cross Country seasons. You went as yourself, you tell yourself. It's the scariest costume you know.

A Sinner's Guide to Canonization

Sunday school, for me, was actually on a Saturday. Every Saturday morning at 9 am, a perfect speed bump to the weekend. 9am was too early to be alive on the weekends. 9 am was when nine year-old me wanted to be watching *Recess* on ABC's "One Saturday Morning".

Instead I was in my pjs in the parish center, a building with cardboard colored walls and the permeating stench of stale coffee, staring at Mrs. Costello's cankles. If Mrs. Costello had ever smiled, I think it had to have been during the old testament, a time that had never been recorded in modern history, a time long before she ever started teaching catechism. She had been on forced sabbatical for a year after showing us graphic abortion photos in the name of scaring us out of sin. Those slides slid somewhere into my bones, sunk their teeth into my dreams. I was what my mother liked to call "skittish." I'd wake my mother up with nightmares about infant limbs, torn and bodiless crawling after me in the dark. I was constantly encountering evil at church school that I had not yet known in life. Catholics have a bizarre habit of forgiving but not forgetting and Mrs. Costello was allowed back, unsupervised and unquestioned.

We were sunk in the bleak season of lent when Mrs. Costello was talking to us about the crucifixion. At this point in my life, I was certain that the actual crucifixion would have been less painful than listening to her talk about it.

"And Mary Magdalene was there too," she droned.

"Isn't that Jesus's Mommy?" I asked, always the interrupter, hand raised and mouth opened before permission was ever granted. I was the bane of Mrs. Costello's existence, the thorn in her side, the way she was mine.

"No Liza," she half scolded, half corrected.

"Than who even is this lady?" I asked, my nine-year-old self befuddled that more than

one person could have the same name.

Mrs. Costello spoke Mary's name in a careful tone, as if the syllables were made of porcelain. Mrs. Costello told us what her teachers before her had whispered about Mary, in that same too careful tone. The centuries had not been kind to Mary. She had the worst reputation, but the prettiest face in my illustrated children's bible. She was also the page Mama was always most likely to skip.

**

Papere proposed to Mamere in a church parking lot in the backseat of Gran Papere's pick up truck, and it wasn't his idea. Mamere's grandfather had helped build this place of worship, a decadent cathedral in the middle of nowhere Maine. Its pillars loomed like the arms of a giant who was taking its time deciding whether or not it would be worth it to eat you whole. The roof slunk on its support beams, bowed and breathing as a whale's rib cage. Between the stained glass panels, Mamere had once found sanctuary. Now, all she could see reflected in the glass was the cold eyes of Saints— those who had never done anything wrong, and those who never would. A stone statue of the Virgin Mary, smooth and flawless and frigid in the October snow glared at Mamere from the churchyard.

"You fucked up," Mary's virgin lips seemed to scorn. "And now you gotta deal with the consequences."

Mamere slid a palm protectively across her stomach. The baby that would be my dad kicked back. Mamere's dad sat in the front seat, his knuckles white on the steering wheel. He'd had enough of Papere's beer cans and his cigarettes and his staring. Never working. Always staring, at people in cars going by, going places he would never go because ambition was something Papere ever seemed to grasp. Granpapere could never understand this. At Papere's age, Granpapere had fought in WWII, had written letters to a woman across an ocean that he promised to marry. This man in his backseat could not even hold a job, did not wish to hold his daughter's hand, even though she was holding his child.

To everyone else, Papere looked like a neanderthal, his forehead too big, sloping into nowhere, his nose too arrowhead, too sharp for his face to ever look anything but mean. He is a collection of all the features Indian women fear their babies will contract. To Mamere, Papere looked like Elvis. Mamere was the type of woman that would only become beautiful in old age, at twenty she was too rounded, with an aristocratic nose and a too soft voice. Every other boy had ignored her, until she met her rockstar, her Jesus, her Patrick. And now there was a possibility that he might stay for good.

"If you leave with him," Granpapere warned. "Then you can never come back."

Mamere spun Papere's class ring around her shaking fingers. She could feel the sting of Mary's gaze from across the lot, reminding her of how much further from holy she was about to go.

"I'll make it work, Daddy. Even if it kills me."

***

Mama warned me Adam would come back for me.

"He shouldn't be texting you," she said. "Boys don't text for no good reason."

I'd protest and say that our past had been laid to rest. Dead as a doornail. He had a girlfriend now. I was smarter now. I tried to ignore the fact that we'd been off and on for nearly three years since we were both college Freshmen. I knew I deserved better now after Matt. I thought I understood now that if you were getting more headaches than orgasms out of a relationship, it probably wasn't working. I silently tallied Adam's sins against me, even made a Word Document about it. When I think about him, I try to see his six foot frame puking in the corner of my dorm room. I try to see his cigarette stained fingers looping around the waist of my best friend. I make a grocery list of betrayals and try to commit it to memory.

But I can't. Instead, I see his wide, grave dirt eyes. He has the eyes of the lost, of the damned. His pupils plead for the help he is too proud to ask for. I see all the times he had ever saved me from myself. How he let me borrow his shoes when I could no longer walk in mine, when a night left me too tipsy for heels. He had been the only one to ever look me dead in the eye and tell me to "slow down, kid." I had this habit of making my life into a bad Lana Del Rey song, acting as if I was just a character in a story I was writing, no feelings, no consequences. He was the only one who ever bothered to see this, to make sure I got home alright. Codependence was our bread and butter. Enablement was the oxygen we shared, even when we were not exactly each other's problems anymore.

He was what I would always stumble back to when I was wounded, as I found myself that Fall in the wreckage of the Incident. Adam was my first, way back in Freshman year, when everything was simpler. He had never really gone away, he remained an ever present specter, an ever-nagging-maybe in the back of my mind. I didn't ask him how he felt about me. Pressing the matter and losing him would be an act akin to carving out my own liver; bloody and not something I was sure I could survive.

Each buzz of my phone felt like the shift of a Ouija board. I didn't know how to explain to mom that you don't start playing with ghosts unless you are looking to summon the dead.

***

In the stories we heard, Mary Magdalene had done something bad. Us kids weren't old enough to know what that was yet. Most adults were too chicken to tell us. I asked Mom once. She told me Mary had "kissed a lot of guys." I didn't understand why this was bad. Mary seemed to have it made. Mary was living the dream. But apparently not?

In the stories we heard, Mary had threadbare clothes and a threadbare face that barely had enough material left to cover the nameless sin she carried around with her. She strolled the streets of Galilee with bare feet. Her hair cascaded down her back in an act of defiance. Proper ladies didn't wear their hair like that. She was the cautionary tale that mothers of the time warned their daughters against becoming. She glared back at these crones unapologetically. She loved unapologetically. Until one day she found a love worth trading for an apology.

***

Daddy grew up in a trailer. Papere was always working nights, Mamere working days; the sun and the moon switching off shifts, only eclipsing for a few moments. And you know what they say about eclipses, sometimes they can mean the end of the world.

Daddy had to be real quiet during the day. If Papere woke up, there'd be hell to pay. The trailer only had one big window. Daddy would stand in front of it, trying to imagine that the trailer had wheels and that him and Mamere could roll far away from there, sometime in the night when Papere was at work. They'd roll all the way to Maine, where his grandparents lived, on the farm where there was space to make as much noise as you wanted. Papere's yelling wouldn't reach them there. No matter how much he drank, he would never be able to get loud enough to reach them there. Mamere's ever-thinning shoulders wouldn't shake from the sound, wouldn't shake when his hand got too close to her skin. Mamere and Daddy would roll right past the little shrine of the Virgin Mary in the garden and on to heaven, somewhere up North.

"Mama, let's go, let's leave while he's at work tonight," my eight-year-old father would beg, the hem of his mother's shirtsleeve white knuckled in his fist.

Mamere would get a far away look in her eye, her eyes always coming to rest on the Mary in the yard.

"We have to make it work, somehow," she'd say. *Even if it kills us.*

***

"What's your name again?" Adam asks, his words slurring from what I'm sure is more than alcohol. My face stings as if I've been slapped. We had become a tradition at this point, three years in a row, coming to find each other every fall since Freshman year. He'd found me in my new apartment, in my new room. We are sitting side by side on my twin bed like strangers on a city bus seat, but naked. There's incense smoke spooling up from my desk, a self portrait on my easel all hollow eyed and cigarette mouthed. I am always frightened at how old I look in paint. I can hardly breathe.

After all this time, he'd still pull shit like pretending to forget my name. He blinks at me like an Alzheimer's patient and I'm struggling to remember what we're both doing here. I blame it on the booze. I blame it on his drugs. I blame it on the fact that it's 3 am. I blame myself for thinking that he was the answer now, that he could be the one to fill this all consuming lonely that had plagued me since the Incident. I blame myself for the greedy way I know his problems are easier to deal with than my own. I blame the way that lying beneath some other girl's man makes it feel as though I deserved all that had happened to me. Because sometimes, all those things are easier to swallow than the truth, that I might not mean as much to him as he does to me.

"Liza," I say.

"Stupid," I think, but don't say out loud.

"That's good, at least I can remember your name," he says.

I wonder whether he can even recall his own name. Or his girlfriend's.

"Does she know you're here?" I ask. He blinks back with the eyes of a child lost in a super Walmart.

"I don't even know where she is," he confesses and it's one of the saddest sentences I've ever heard, even though I hate her guts. I hate her purely because she has him. He leans down to kiss me, with the thought of her still on his tongue. He tastes like cigarette butts and Jack Daniels.

"I've been drinking since Thursday," he says when he pulls away. It's Sunday now. This was something I was used to. He'd ramble off the things he'd done in the past week, and I'd nod along silently, without judgment or interruption. Sometimes I'd make a Word Document of the things he'd told me he'd taken or drank. This way, if he ever did need to go to the emergency room, at least someone would know what to tell the doctors. At least someone would be left with the truth. "I haven't been to class in three days."

I wonder if his girlfriend listens to him like this. I pray to a God I no longer believe in all the time that she talks him down at the end of his list. I've been praying for a lot of things lately. I don't pray for her to leave him though. I love him too much for that.

***

Mary washed Jesus's feet with her loose, unladylike hair. She kissed each toe in turn. She promised to love Him, only Him. The apostles whispered about her "bad name" behind her back. She shot them glares. She had perfected and invented the "dirty look". She repented. She gave up many loves for one. This, Mrs. Costello told us, made Mary Magdalene a saint.

When Jesus was crucified, His apostles ran, they denied Him, they betrayed Him. Mary watched each nail sink into His skin. Mary held her love's lifeless body in her arms. She buried Him. She didn't understand what all this sacrifice was for, but she stood by Him to the end. And for all her faithfulness, she was the first to see Him rise from the dead. For all her loyalty, He came back to her, and proclaimed her royalty.

Mary has sat in silence as centuries have took their turn with her, painting her as whore, prostitute and worse. Mary sought refuge in her faith, when in the end it was the thing that destroyed her. Mrs. Costello got it wrong. This, I argue, is what made Mary Magdalene a saint.

***

When I was five-years-old, Papere threw a chair at Mamere in hospice. He was mad because she was sick of putting up with his shit, and told him so. A dying woman has nothing to lose, especially with a staff of nurses to back her. She would be dead from cancer in a week. Papere didn't want her to leave him, even if it was in death. Papere had to leave. Mamere never got the chance to.

At her wake, I got a Hawaiian Barbie to keep me quiet during the service. I got the Virgin Mary statue from Mamere's garden, too; it was supposed to keep me brave. I held both these idols in my tiny hands looking over the lip of the casket at what had been my grandmother. Holding fast to these three ways to be a woman— the virgin, the whore, the human—I wondered, even then, how I was supposed to juggle all three without falling, without dropping something. Mamere was pretty in death the way she had never been in youth. Still and quiet, she was now as thin as she had always wanted to be. The funeral hall I was standing in would be converted to a liquor store within the span of a year. My father would buy Jack Daniels from a counter they erected in the space his mother's casket once occupied. I would never wonder why he could never drink enough to forget.

Papere got her life insurance and all her investments. A few months later he found a girlfriend that looked a lot like Mamere, especially in the way her shoulders shook when Papere was around. Daddy didn't get anything but grief.

We buried her in the churchyard under a gravestone meant for two. Mamere's dates are all filled in, all fifty years. Papere's name is there, but we're still waiting on a day. Daddy says it will be a while though, he says that evil lives forever. Daddy puts a bunch of daisies next to Mamere's name every spring, for what used to be her Birthday.

"Your Mamere was a saint," Daddy tells me with the tight voice men use because they're not allowed to cry, at least not in front of their daughters. I wince. I realize a saint is not something I ever want to be.

***

"Can you walk me out?" Adam asks because no matter how wasted, he never spends the night. I slide on a shirt while Adam pulls his jeans on over his socks. He never takes his socks off. He'll admit that he has an issue with feet. We're both just a little too afraid to be completely naked around anybody, me with my earrings and him with his socks. I dangle the pack of Camels he left on my desk in front of his face so he remembers to take them with him. I don't need that brand of temptation under my roof.

"Of course I'll walk you out," I tell him, because what else am I gonna say?

"Thanks, Liza. You're a saint," he says. I give him a dirty look, the look I reserve for people who are BS-ing me.

"Uh… I don't know about that, dude," I protest. He shrugs.

"Well, you're a saint to me," he says.

The rest of the apartment is dark. I don't dare flip on the light for fear of waking my roommates. Its too early in the morning to have to explain myself. We stub our toes and curse at every turn through the blackened kitchen towards the fire escape. He fumbles in his pocket for a light. The tiny lighter is enough to guide us to the door.

"See, smoking comes in handy sometimes," he says.

I don't argue because it's not my responsibility to save him from himself anymore. That's supposed to be his girlfriend's job. I can't afford to be this invested. I have enough of my own problems now. I don't understand what his self-destruction is for, and it's not my place to ask. I fling open the front door. He pulls me in for a goodbye kiss, territory we've never trod before. And then another. And another. I forget about his girl across town. I forget that I might be letting the cat out. I forget that my roommate will kill me if the cat goes missing. I forget to fear what will happen if this cat gets let out of the bag. I think to myself, that maybe, this is all that heaven is— a proper goodbye.

But then, he is gone, stumbling down the sidewalk, back to campus, to find her. His six foot frame looks so small with the streetlights pressing down on it. I wonder how something that looks so small could have possibly fucked up my life this badly. I seek refuge in his arms even though time and time again, he is what destroys me. It will take me six months to get over this, and by that time he will be back again. Heartbreak is a stigmata for me; I wear it on my sleeve until he returns. I turn on all the lights. I watch him until he's gone from my view and once again gone from my life. Because that's the saddest thing about saints; they can never really call anything their own.

How to Forget

It is New Year's Eve, a night for burying the dead, burying the hatchet, planting something new. You pick up Matt, an old lover, and an even older friend, on your way home from Connecticut. You convince yourself this will be worth it, even though it adds two extra hours to your trip. You pick Olly up too, a skinny, twitchy fucker who you introduce to strangers as your brother. This is a 'family' reunion in the dead of winter. This is an old house resettling its bones. This is an old cast with a new script. You spend the car ride hoping that you can remember the right words.

You spend the car ride listening to Olly's self titled mix tapes: *blowjob party mix, shit spill fumble fuck,* a train wreck of Indie voices crooning *please don't go, I love you so* and D12 rapping about the rules of pimping. You spend the car ride listening to Matt mansplain acid, something you have no intention of ever taking. He believes himself prophet because he reached "ego-death" over the fall. You want to explain that you've been to ego-death too, this is what happens when your lover's girlfriend comes after you on social media during finals. You feel even smaller than you did in October, your Band-Aid had only infected the wound. This is not a story for your ex. You think his head's too big for the car.

You watch the December skeleton trees, reaching futile but silently for the sky out your windshield. You are envious of them for a moment, the way they are so sure their roots will hold, year after year, standing in the same place, stretching towards the same heaven. You will never have that luxury, you are not a tree, your roots were excavated years ago.

You go home, put a pizza in the oven. You burn it horribly. It's ok, no one really planned on eating it anyway. You take a shower, change into a little black dress. When you walk out of your room, Matt will groan and ask why you couldn't have kept your flannel on. He will ask why you couldn't have just been one of the bros for the night. You will realize he is saying this because it is easier for him to accept you as only a friend when you are dressed like a trucker and not like the way he remembers you from last summer. He looks the same as when you visited in the Fall, but you no longer feel the same. His pug nose rests too big on his skull now, his hair is longer and clown wild. He is the Jonah Hill sidekick to your romantic comedy now. You have come to accept this, even if he hasn't.

You start drinking at 4 pm to cut the awkward tension that has settled over the apartment. You start with blowjob shots, an oozing brain of whipped cream peeking over the top of your crystal skull shot glass. These taste like sugar coated battery acid, but the name suits you, so you choke it back. You wipe the foam from the corner of your mouth. You never complain.

The party you planned begins at 8. By the time it rolls around you are too drunk to remember who you invited. Matt reminds you constantly to "sit like a lady" in your skin tight black dress. You tell him to go fuck himself, which has more to do with every way he has ever broken your heart than the words he is actually saying now.

Olly is in over his head, drunk out of his skull. He asks the only two black people at the party if they are twins. He hits on your straight friend, Glen, relentlessly, to the point that after this night, whenever Glen is invited to anything, he will give you a deer in the headlights expression and ask, "Is Olly going to be there?"

Olly kisses you full on the mouth while you are sitting, very unlike a "lady", on top of the heater. You punch him in the face so hard your knuckles ache from the impact. Tomorrow bruises will flower up along the back of your hand, the only type of garden you have ever tended. It will make you think of getting banned from the school bus as a child for winning too often at "bloody knuckles," a game that hinges on punching someone else's hand until the loser screams "mercy." You think of all the ways your strength has always been measured in what you can endure silently.

The boy from your writing class shows up, the goofy looking one with the Cheech and Chong hat and the too small face. He had made out with you in November, outside a cross country party, while that year's first snow dusted your shoulders. That night he had pulled away, saying he respected you as a writer. You stood in the accumulating snow as the black line of his back disappeared past the view of the streetlights. You wonder about how the word "respect" sits like the burning end of a cigarette in the pit of your stomach. It feels warmer than the word "love" ever did. You think maybe this boy will be different. He won't be.

Later in your room, on a comforter printed with letters, while a party goes on without you outside your door, you will remember that this boy has read you compare other lovers to Jesus. Perhaps this is what he is after when he kisses you, when he peels your dress over your shoulders while clocks are striking midnight elsewhere. Not to keep you, but the chance to be described as something worthy of divinity.

In the weeks after this, when his text messages slow to a trickle and then die out in a drought, you will make a vow to yourself that you will never give him what he came there looking for. You will never write a story about him. You will never describe him as anything but what he was, a thief with a mouth full of pretty words.

But on that night, the two of you reappear from your room into the new year like nothing happened. Olly throws up in your roommate's watering can. All the other guests have left, but you do not notice this until the boy from your writing class kisses you goodbye for the first and last time. The boy cups your ass like he is Atlas holding up the world. You smile, amazed that somebody out there is still amazed by you. You sing Auld Lang Syne absently to yourself as his footfalls echo down your fire escape. *Shall old acquaintance be forgot and never brought to mind.*

Matt, too sober for his own good, has witnessed everything, like Nick Carraway observing a Gatsby party. He sits you and Olly down at the kitchen table like an angry parent spewing lecture into the light of your afterglow. You can't look Matt in the eye so you're staring at your folded hands where they rest on the ink splattered surface of the table. At some point during the night, you or someone else had managed to scrawl the word "slut" across your forearm in angry red sharpie. The word screams at you now, an accusation from your own skin. You wonder absently if this mark was the only thing the boy saw while you were fucking him, you wonder absently if he ever saw beyond it. If anyone can anymore.

"The decisions you guys make while you're drunk still exist in the morning, you know," Matt tells you. You want to tell him that all too often, they don't. That the only trace is your weight weary memory and the stack of journals on your bedroom floor. You want to ask him if that's something he can promise, if anybody can anymore.

A Nomad's Guide to Home Ownership

Before the Incident, June, summer camp, staff lounge

"It's time to get up," I tell Matt. Light is cracking through the skylight, cracking open our eyelids like eggshells so he shuts his again, dreamingly, ignoring me. We've been sleeping on a puddle of blankets and pillows stolen from different corners of camp, and pooled onto the staff lounge floor. The body pillows and tattered quilts we are laying on vaguely smell like children; piss, maple syrup, sour patch kids. The lounge is the upper floor of the day camp area, a box TV and ribbons of VHS tapes are sprawled out in the corner. An audience of mismatched and understuffed recliners are the only ones to bear witness to what has happened here.

If we are going to continue to keep this relationship private, we are going to need to get out of here before anybody else wakes up. We don't want anybody to know. At least this is what I tell myself, because this is what Matt wants. I have learned by now to not ask for definitions for what boys' hands reach for in the dark. I have learned enough by now to know that being somebody's dirty secret is better than being their nothing.

Matt was and is my friend first. A boy with a pug nose, small blue eyes and a skull spewing blond curls. An Aryan, he jokes all the time. It makes me cringe, thinking of my grandfather's doctored Ellis Island last name, thinking of all the Indian in my cheek bones. I fell for Matt's personality, never his face. I still have to close my eyes when I kiss him.

I count his imperfections like rosary beads, each one a saving grace, proving that he is just flawed enough for me to hope to keep. He is a type of ugly that is within my reach, a type that I can't imagine ever breaking my heart.

I scramble to gain my footing to get up from our makeshift bed on the floor, but Matt sweeps me off my feet again. He pulls me in close to his chest and squeezes me so tight that I feel my walls breaking and maybe part of my skeleton too. I worry that my foundation will crack, that I will need him to support me. Then right when I feel as though I'm about to burst, he puts a bow on it by kissing the back of my neck. This is where I live, at the intersection between his mouth and my neck. This is home.

"This isn't getting up," I mumble, playing at being annoyed.

"No it's not," he says, without moving a muscle. He knows my address, because he lives here too.

***

Junior year, March, nowhere downtown LA

I feel like I'm walking on eggshells clicking down the LA sidewalk in freshly broken in heels. Two other writers and I are headed back to our hotel from a conference. A conference that will tell us how to better say our own words in print. I am wary of this advice. I am a person uncertain of everything except what I want to write and how I want to write it. I am always out for the blood of anyone who tells me that I do this wrong. Criticism has never been something I've taken lightly, regardless of my devil-may-care attitude.

We are now hopelessly lost in nowhere, LA. Our hotel seems to have grown legs and moved to the suburbs to raise a family, as sick of the hustle and bustle as I am. It's been three hours of circles. Bianca, Olivia and I have lost our direction. I am losing my patience. I can feel layers of my soles peeling back beneath the thin skin of my fishnets. Bianca and

Olivia are staring at the GPS, and have not realized how far behind I'm trailing. Bianca has never been to this city, but she's acting like it's her hometown, the blind giving directions to the blind.

Back home, I live with Bianca in a half-broken college apartment. My patience with her dirty dish and clogged drain ways are thin ice I'm trying to keep from crashing through. Even the sight of her unwashed brown hair bordering her expensive Patagonia sweatshirt grates on my every nerve. Her family is wealthy, an ancestor of her's invented the dentist's chair or something and she benefits from the only trickle down system I've ever seen work in person. I am swiftly realizing that she is everything about Connecticut that I have tried to move away from. She has the means to do anything with her life that she wishes, but she can't even be bothered to shampoo her own hair. Her privilege is a toy in the palm of her hand. She will never understand where I come from, where I am or where I am going, but ironically enough she is barking back directions to me at the crossroads of every street. This trip marks the beginning of the hairline fractures that will inevitably shatter our friendship.

But now, I am just trying to bite my tongue, to not swear down the sidewalk. At least not in front of Olivia, a girl with a mouth that always looks like it's posed to say "fuck you." Olivia and I had never been friends, I crossed too many lines in my life for that to ever be the case, but we respect each other, in writing, in feminism, in all the ways we talk about love and those who did not love us. I don't want to change that, so I dry swallow my temper.

With each turn by Bianca's hand we are pulled further into the labyrinth of downtown LA. I am limping behind in a poor fashion choice. I am a walking wounded, looking up with weary eyes, trying to find the hotel room that we are temporarily calling home, but every skyscraper looks the same. I am praying to a god I no longer believe in to deliver us home.

***

The 90's, Liza's childhood home

When I was young, before I knew better (or rather before I knew any worse), I believed what my mother's bible told me. Momma would read to me from the illustrated children's edition every night. The drawings were simple, but the stories were the same brutal murders, betrayals that I overheard from the pulpit each Sunday. My favorite story was of Exodus (or "exorcist", as my five-year-old brain pronounced it). The tale of Moses leading his people to freedom. Cartoon slaves were strewn about the pages like road kill. "Deliver us," said their speech bubbles. I traced the letters I was too young to read. "Deliver me."

***

Before the Incident, August, summer camp, residential cabin

Matt pulls away from me. He sits naked on the edge of the bunk bed mattress as if it were a cliff he was considering jumping off of. The moon is spilling in through my cracked cabin window making him look pale, like he's a corpse already. He puts his head in his hands, because right now this is easier than looking at me. Because whatever is going on in his brain is too heavy for just his neck to support. He looks so small, so helpless, like a child thrown awake from a nightmare.

"What's wrong?" I ask. I scootch so that my thigh lines up with his. I trace all the things I cannot say to him aloud in invisible cursive across the ball of his shoulder. He shifts just far enough to be out of my reach.

"I don't think I can put it into words," he says. And suddenly, neither can I. I comb my vodka scattered mind for a reason, a word of comfort to make him stay. But my search comes up with nothing. Nothing but this silence hanging like an impatient guillotine blade above our heads. The end is near, we can hear the wind hissing against the edge of it. But maybe that's just the ocean breeze battering the windows of the cabin.

Death hangs heavy in this cabin, I am alone here for the weekend, for the rest of the summer, forever. My co-counselor, a soft spoken girl with glasses and a pixie cut had fled. She had had a miscarriage in the dining hall bathroom during siesta the other day. She hadn't even known she was pregnant until her baby was already dead, staring up at her like some warped Halloween decoration from the crisp white porcelain of the toilet bowl. She told me she was sorry, but she couldn't stay, couldn't sleep here beside me anymore. The nightmares were too harsh here. My coworker, my only female friend at camp, was gone before I could even think of a way to tell her anything more useful than I'm sorry. And now I just feel haunted in this cabin, haunted for what leaves us without cause or explanation. Haunted for things we don't even know we have to lose, until it's too late.

Sitting here with Matt in this standoff shooting silence, the back of my skull feels as though it has a bullet in it. I have Lyme disease, from spending a summer in a tent with him, but I don't know this yet. All I know is that five minutes have gone by without a word being passed between us, or a look or even the brushing of skin. Through the silence I hear a sound, not a real one, but a screaming of quiet that rings through my ears like the funeral taps I once heard echoing across the harbor outside this cabin. This is dying. We are dying.

I'm the first to move. I'm scrambling for my t-shirt on the cabin floor. Not because I'm cold, but because of a sudden need to cover up. It suddenly seems very wrong that I am naked in front of him, even though this is mostly how I have spent the past three months. When I pull my head through my shirt, I know he is feeling the same way too because in the split second it took me to navigate my tangled mind through a crop top, he has zipped up his jeans, buckled belt and all.

"I don't think I should stay the night," he says. I stare blankly ahead like someone who's been shot. A drawer rolls loose in my mind, memories spilling everywhere like marbles. It's a collection of goodbyes he has given me for safekeeping over the summer. I pick each one up gingerly and examine it in the fading light. Him squeezing me tighter and kissing the back of my neck. Him kissing the outline of my thigh on the way out of our tent. These were not goodbyes at all, but promises, a promise to return because we had left something unfinished.

Now he doesn't even turn back to kiss me on the way out the door. No more promises. He became one of the ghosts he battled with each time he held me, the shadows of those who came before him. I hope he is proud now, to be among their ranks. I am left staring out between the broken shutters of a haunted house.

***

Junior year, March, tent city, downtown LA

This is the third time Bianca, Olivia and I have circled the block, an interstate bridge cross hatched over half-erected tarp residences. Skyscrapers gleam like broken teeth in the sun, ugly and proud. The air smells like Mexico, tortillas frying and chilies drying in the heat. A palm tree is choke hold planted in concrete. This is the city of angels, but I can't hear God here.

The residents of the local tent city have taken notice of our caravan. They are shirtless, grizzled, shoeless. Their beards stretch from their faces like run on sentences. Black, white, Chinese, Mexican, we have stumbled upon the United Nations of poverty. Everyone is equal here. They are modge-podged lions licking their chops, pinning me as the weakest of the herd. I can feel their eyes crawling up the back of my slip skirt, their gaze weaving in and out the windows of my fishnet stockings.

"Where ya going baby?" they call. *I don't even know.*

"You lost sweetheart?" they hiss. *For all of my life.*

Tears are pricking at the backs of my eyes. The sun is going down, giving up on us. What will we do when night swallows up the sidewalk? We are three women, three girls really, from a small college town in nowhere Maine.

This city is the real world. In the real world, things happened to you that were not your own fault. Girls disappeared all the time out here, swallowed up by the desert sand or drowned in the Pacific ocean. Crime shows written for CBS or TNT take place on these streets. And how many episodes begin with the narrow silhouette of a twenty-something-year-old girl lined in chalk? How many episodes begin with a pretty blonde head being zipped into a body bag? TV and life prove to us again and again that pretty girls are more beautiful when they can no longer talk back. The tragic will always be sexier than the powerful.

We are in Manson's state. Anything could happen, especially to the lost. My face is crumpling, a scared little kid yelling down the aisles of a supermarket for a lost parent. But we are orphans here and my voice is lost between the shelves of skyscrapers and canvas tents.

***

After the Incident, February, living room floor, Liza's apartment

Matt messages me out of the brittle winter blue.

"Yo, Liza, Where we at after last summer?"

Outside my apartment window, snowflakes are falling like dandruff, the sky is chafing and rubbing me in all the wrong ways. I am still learning how to be cold. I was just minding my own business, watching *Life* with the roomies on the floor of the living room and now I'm being thrown into a quarter life crisis. I can't keep the room from spinning like a merry-go-round beneath my feet. I want to burrow my way into the shag carpet I am laying on and never come out. I feel like my next breath depends on me answering this text. Where had my best friend left me after a summer of hookups? How could I explain that I am not the same person anymore? That too much had happened to this body since he last left it? What is a polite way to explain that the hallway of his dorm building shows up in all of my nightmares?

I'm staring at the phone as if it's a dead body. Mercy's peering her chicken skinny neck over my shoulder from her perch on the futon. She watches our lives like it's a MTV reality show, scripted especially for her entertainment. She twirls one of her pearl earrings around with a twig thin finger. She always wears pearls, while running, while chilling at home, the way I always wear a full face of makeup. It always looks as though she is wedding ready, I always look fuck ready. People tell you to dress for the job you want, we dress for the lives we expect, but not necessarily the ones we desire for ourselves.

"Is everything ok?" Mercy asks. She is sitting comfortably, if not awkwardly in the embrace of her live-in boyfriend, Robbie, a small Mexican looking runner who is shorter than she is. They are an odd pair, but it's still the type of cute that makes me cringe, makes me homesick for something I've never had. I can't bear to look at them for too long.

I show Mercy the phone screen. She shrieks, like she does when she sees or hears something she can't quite believe. I cover my ear with my free hand.

"Well what do you think?" she asks. As if this is simple. As if this is a multiple choice question and not the diffusing of a bomb.

"I will always love him, but I can't like him anymore," is my response. She throws her hand over her mouth in shock like I had just got engaged or some sappy shit like that.

"Aw! Liza!" she squeals with the frequency of a jet plane taking off. "So you're going to end up with Matt?!"

She is so relieved to have me sorted out. I nod along because it is easier to adopt her childlike view of the world— that there is a cause for every effect, and the world owes you a happily ever after. That the world owes you a place to call home.

I see that if my drunken wishes to a genie in a bottle of Jack were to come true, it had nothing to do with me.

"We're bros, right?" I text back, I don't know what else to say to him. I loved you and we destroyed each other? We were at each other's throats each night, trying to see who would suffocate first. That I'd do anything to be left that breathless again. I hold my breath and type;

"But that doesn't mean you're completely friend-zoned."

"You don't have to sleep on the floor when you come visit Saturday then," he says. Just like that, I'm back on the inside. I stare at my phone, as if a scorpion had come to rest in my palm. It's deadly and calculating. It's going to kill me, but I don't know when.

***

The pages of Liza's illustrated bible

Moses's mama was a slave lady in the shadow of the pyramids, in the shadow of Pharaoh's hand, poised above them like the tail of a scorpion, ready to strike if he ever got spooked. And the Israelites did spook him with their large numbers. Pharaoh tossed and turned at night with nightmares of an impending rebellion. Pharaoh kept the population in check by throwing Hebrew baby boys to the crocodiles.

Moses's mother knew to keep her baby was to sentence him to death. She decided to put him up for adoption, by bundling him in a basket and sending him down the river. At this point in the story, I would always look up at my mother, a woman with a Jennifer Grey beautiful face that I would spend my whole life adding nothing but worry lines to. "Mama, how did Moses' mommy know he was gonna be ok?" I'd ask.

"She didn't," She would say, in a voice meant for an adult, not a five-year-old. "Women have to make all the tough choices. Sometimes they're right and sometimes they're wrong. But all our choices are the hardest."

I would pout, even at five, I had little patience for the possibility of my life being anything but easy, anything but a blessed fairy tale. But I kept my ears open.

God delivered Moses through the teeth of crocodiles and around the jaws of hippopotamuses to the front stoop of the palace. Pharaoh's wife scooped up the baby, thanking her gods for delivering him to her. "He is a blessing," she told Pharaoh. What she didn't know is that he was an enemy.

Family secrets never stay hidden for long. Moses grew up and learned the truth. In a fit of teen angst, he fled Egypt. He moved in with some nomads, met a nice girl, started leading some sheep around. The boy was finally living the dream, finally free, finally home and then God does what God does best; He fucked up Moses' life.

***

After the Incident, February, Matt's dorm room,
some college that is not mine

Matt and I bundle the smoke detector in his dorm in Hannaford's take away bags. We decide this isn't sufficient. We wring our hands over the exhalations of vapes, blunts and cigs. We joke half-heartedly about the fire department showing up outside the window and bumming a light. We joke about the residential assistant coming to the door while we are blasting "Fuck the Police" through the speakers.

The laughter goes out like a cigarette butt on the sidewalk. We cinch a backpack around the Hannaford's bag like a noose. We've killed our guilt, at least when it comes to the smoke detector. Now we're choking on nicotine that tastes like Watermelon sour patch kids, sucking candy smoke through electronic boxes. Vaping will not kill us, for definite. We're ambiguous on the side effects, ambiguous on everything. We're drunk and freezing because we're keeping the windows cracked cross breeze style as a triple precaution.

Matt's dorm looks the same as it had in October, when I was last here. The same cringe worthy posters, weed strains and psychedelic designs, are draped across the cinder block walls. Matt's desktop computer still groans like a pet monster from the floor and table of his desk, always open to Spotify. I've never heard anything but music here, we've never been comfortable with silence. The graveyard of bottles has gotten bigger now, sprawling across the floor and edging it's way out from his closet like the hand of a zombie from a coffin. The yogibo is gone. Dio dropped out and dragged it home with her. I say it's too bad that this is gone now, talking more about the girl than the bean bag chair.

I'm sitting on Matt's roommate's bed, with a boy on either side, neither worthy of me. I am a lonely queen. The boy on the left does not look like he is old enough to be in college, sand blonde hair and a too-round face. But he gives the best back massages, and I allow him this much. The boy on the right is tall, dark haired with gauges just big enough for me to stick my pinky through.

"Aren't they dope?" the boy asks me, clasping a disfigured earlobe between two fingers.

"I've seen bigger," I say in a voice that drips innuendo, but it goes over his head. He is not smart enough to see that I am making fun of all the ways he tries and fails to perform toughness for me.

Matt is sitting in a spinny chair, purposely on his lonesome. I'm plotting maniacally to make my way over there, to escape this stale flirting and get the night rolling. I had spent the entire week remembering, trying to relearn Matt's mouth, his arms. I am so close I can taste him, but there is still six feet and an ocean between us. I am getting impatient. I am getting anxious. He told me not to bring my sleeping bag, told me that I could sleep with him, but now he doesn't seem interested.

I'm terrified that I'm going to have to sleep in my car. It's below thirty out. I'll get frostbite, someone will tap on my window in the morning to find me as frozen and beautiful as Sleeping Beauty. I'll get abducted. I'll get arrested. I'll forget to pull the emergency brake and wake up at the bottom of a hill.

I will not be a hobo, not even on a temporary basis. Nor will I stoop so low as to bang the baby faced Freshman tracing calligraphy into my thigh or the overly emotional Junior with the gauges running his fingers through my hair, in the name of a place to sleep.

"You're hot," Baby Face whispers in my ear.

"I know," I say.

I am better than this.

This opinion drops unwarranted on my lap. Nothing I have ever done suggests that this is true. Who am I to say I was worth more than this? Impulsive confidence and stupid pride.

I lick my fangs and go in for the kill. I fling myself up off the mattress, handing my red solo cup of Jack to Gauges with the tenderness of someone handing their baby to a sitter. My head spins mobiles, and my fishnet bound feet walk an unsteady tightrope across the linoleum floor towards Matt. His eyes spread wide, like I'm oncoming traffic when he sees where I'm headed. He slides the vape onto the desk, pulls his hands to the armrests as if bracing for impact.

I expect to hear screeching metal when we meet, the sound of planets aligning, a universe creaking to a halt. But all I can hear are heartbeats, his and mine, too loud and unsure. I don't think I've ever actually sat on anybody's lap before, but now I've got my ass on Matt's knee. We slip into a casual intimacy. I'm home with my hands around his neck. It's like I never left. It makes me question why I ever did. Everything else about my life that doesn't revolve around my tongue down his throat seems irrelevant, a waste of time.

But we can't commit to this. There are other people here, and what we were was never anything public. He slaps me on the ass and sends me back to my throne with love, so he can play with his vape. He blows smoke through his nose like a dragon, a false monster, all smoke and no fire. I think coward, I think sneak, but I don't know if I am talking about him or me anymore.

Baby Face is biting at my neck the moment my ass hits the bed, his fingers spinning circles into my vertebrae. Gauges challenges me to a chug battle. We toast our solo cups with the solemnity of soldiers headed off to a losing battle. I watch Gauges chug. He is struggling after three sips. I go bottoms up.

"Matt, your girl's insane!" Gauges sputters.

"I know," Matt says, and I smile between the rim of my solo cup, because for once no one stood corrected. He didn't tell Gauges that I am not his girl, that I belong to nothing and no one. Not even to myself and especially not to him. For tonight, at least, I am his.

***

Junior year, March, street corner, downtown LA

Bianca and Olivia pause for a minute to retrace our steps on a street corner, giving me the chance to catch up. I slump my back against a lamp post. I kick off my heels. I rub the stigmata I have carved into the soles of my feet. I think about melting into the sidewalk, disappearing into the ocean of gray beneath my toes. It seems as good a solution as any, a quiet solution. I had always assumed I would be a city girl, small towns talked too much, small towns knew every sin on your soul and gossiped about it in public. But LA is overwhelming, I am a footnote here, I am no one here, nothing I do is shocking here. And I'm beginning to believe that maybe I don't belong anywhere.

The street is some strange river. Mexicanos in wife beaters and hot rods rev their engines, whistle, wink and toss their cigarette butts in my direction. I roll my eyes at their displays... And yet, I chase each car window with my eyes, hungry for the attention. Middle-aged businessmen roll down the backseat windows of their professionally driven cars, they don't say anything, they just breathe me in. A man on a motorcycle gives me a head nod. Makes me think Hunter S Thompson's *Hell's Angels*. Makes me think Kurt Sutter's *Sons of Anarchy*. I consider jumping on the back of his motorcycle. I could be a great old lady to somebody. I already wear just enough leather. This is delusional though and I chalk it up to lonely, I chalk it up to everything and everyone I have left a country away in Maine for the week.

Why do they bother with me? This brief exchange in the span of a stoplight? Nothing will come of it, not a word, not a kiss, nor touch or one night stand. And yet lane after lane, car after car they take their turn to worship at my feet. I am swallowed up in faces, drowned in eyes. I am struggling to find a significance, a narrative amidst the noise of voices screaming through the city void in an attempt to prove that for one glimmering moment, they are not alone.

My soles are screaming at me as I slide my heels back on to continue walking.

"Keep your fucking shoes off!" my feet yell up at me. I have Indian feet; they are only truly happy when they can feel the earth beneath their toes. But the sidewalk reeks of urine. "You can take a shower when you get home.." my toes bargain with me.

"What type of foot fungus could I possibly contract in the span of a few blocks?" I ask myself. The possibilities are endless, the paths are infinite and we have no idea how to get back home.

***

Liza's illustrated bible

God tells Moses he must return to Egypt for his people, that his freedom means nothing if they are still in chains. Moses argues, but does what Daddy says. Pharoah is not so easy to convince. God throws a temper tantrum and sends plague upon plague to Egypt. It rains locusts and frogs. Smallpox bloom like tattoo roses on Egyptian skin. The Holy Ghost eats the souls of every firstborn Egyptian child, including Pharaoh's son. Pharaoh lets Moses and his people go.

This is happily ever after, right? The Hebrews are free! They did it! But now where are they supposed to go? What are they supposed to do? They follow Moses blindly, bumbling around in search of milk and honey. They are alone in the desert, responsible for their own lives for the first time. They are hungry, they are thirsty. They grow weary of the way all the sand, the way the sky and the horizon melt into a miraged infinity.

They question why Moses did this to them. Moses questions God. This is not how freedom was supposed to taste. The Hebrews wander the desert for forty years. Moses will never see the promised land he was promised. He will die without ever knowing if his sacrifice was for good or ruin. He will never make it home.

These were my bedtime stories. I drifted off to sleep with, one dream on my mind. Free. It was the most beautiful word I had ever known. Dear God, please, oh please won't you deliver me? Deliver me home.

***

After the Incident, February, Matt's dorm room, college campus

"We can still do this, if you're still down," Matt offers when people finally vacate. We are sitting on two separate beds, talking into the six foot space separating us. I feel like we will always be this far apart, close enough to touch but achingly parallel in our pursuits.

"Is that even a question?" I ask, because I'm not sure if he's asking or telling me. Dripping from my lips it sounds like a yes, and I suppose I'll go with that.

"Top drawer," he says, with no explanation. It's fine, I already know what he's talking about. I hop off the bed on woozy and uncertain feet. I walk a more or less straight line to his desk, fling open the drawer and retrieve a condom.

I walk over to kiss him and he barely moves from where he is propped up with a pillow on his bed. Kissing him feels like persuasion, like I have to convince him with each touch of my lips that he does want me there, that this was always his idea before it was ever mine. This love affair has always been and perhaps always will be a one sided conversation. And I am getting so tired of always talking to myself.

I thought this would be a homecoming, that maybe I'd understand something about how my life was going. But with him under me, his hands blooming bruises into my hips, I just feel more alone. *Like, this? This is what you were looking for? This skinny boy with a vape down his throat, this is the salvation you were banking on?* On second thought, he don't look a thing like a resurrection. He doesn't look a thing like Jesus, just like The Killers had always said.

When we fall apart, he stares up at the ceiling with the eyes of the dead. I coil my body around his, tracing his bass clef tattoo with a manicured fingernail, trying to bring him back to me, futilely trying to call him home with a pair of tits and a few memories.

He leaves to go puke up fireball and nicotine. Matt's bed is shoved up against a still open window. The February wind bites at my bare skin, but I don't really mind. It reminds me that there are colder things than lukewarm lovers. I peer past the curtains. The moon is peeking through the clouds like it's auditioning for Peter Pan. Clouds scrape the Mary Poppins chimneys of the dorm buildings. The landscape is a fairy tale, but the story has no plot. He has come back to me! But I am nowhere to be found. If I was not waiting for him, then what am I waiting for?

I army crawl closer to the window, letting the moonlight paint my tits a Madonna shade

of divinity. I don't give a fuck if the neighbors can see me, eat your heart out, while you still can, because I'm pretty sure mine got swallowed whole a long time ago. I look down at the sidewalk calculatively. If I jumped, would it be enough to kill me? Shatter my pretty blond skull across the starlit concrete? I've swallowed too much tonight to know that this sounds crazy, concerning. I am just thinking about how lovely it will be when it all just stops. When the quiet welcomes me home like a prodigal daughter.

I'm listening for the sound of Matt gagging through the paper thin walls. If he's still puking, he's still conscious and we can survive the night without anybody getting their stomachs pumped. A better friend would go check on him, but right now I never wanna see his face again. Right now I am still afraid to walk to the bathroom alone. He has no one to blame but himself. I thought this would be a homecoming, but I've never slept in this bed before. This night is an eviction notice. I've paid all the rent I could manage, and now it's time to move on. There's no use in living in houses that are haunted and no love in spooning with the dead.

How to Speak

You spend your spring break drawing a lunar moth in pencil on watercolor paper. The veins of its wings spread like outstretched fingers, hungry and reaching, always wanting more. You ask your mom if the design is any good, your friend Shane is paying you to draw a tramp stamp for her. At least that's what you say out loud. The moth is actually for you, a moth with no mouth. Lunar moths cannot eat, cannot speak. All they can do is fuck and die. You relate to this more days than you don't.

On a Saturday a few weeks later, you drive two hours by yourself to the tattoo parlor. Nobody else wants to go, you have no one for moral support. If you did, maybe you wouldn't be getting a tramp stamp at all. But you don't dwell on this too much; you've always been in love with the romanticism of your own loneliness.

You walk into the shop unannounced and flash your drawing like an admission ticket. You get a three hour wait and a compliment. You go to Starbucks, Urban Outfitters, Mexicali Blues. One book store and then another. You wander Portland like the homeless you see on nearly every street corner, their grime encrusted foreheads crowned with dreadlocks. They hold signs like rosary beads, *desperate, anything will help, hungry, just trying to make it home.* You wonder what your sign should say if you were to have one. You are some kind of lost girl floating around somebody else's city.

A girl you once loved lives in this neighborhood and you spend your afternoon doing what you'd imagine she'd do because you no longer have an understanding of how you like to fill your days. Your pastimes are leftovers shoplifted from other people's personalities. Your days are nothing but an obituary to those who have left you.

The wait time is up. The tattoo artist tells you to sit Indian style on the table. You want to tell him that every way you sit is Indian style, but you don't, you just comply. Your feet fall asleep before you even feel the needle. The tattoo artist will pull passersby over to admire your work, and inadvertently, your midriff, your ass. "Have you ever gotten a tattoo on your lower back?" he'll ask the baddest and the gooniest.

"Nah, too painful," they all say. You want to scream, *no duh*. You want to swear. But you're too busy trying to prove that you can handle this. That this needle biting at your vertebrae is nothing to you. So you clench your teeth a little tighter, dig your fingernails a little deeper into the plastic cushioning of the table. And you smile like it's Christmas morning, you smile like a bride, you smile like a lunatic. You are tough. You can hang. You belong here.

When the tattoo is complete, the artist will take a picture of it for his Facebook page. He is impressed with your design. With the way you "took that like a man." You shrug it off and listen to him rattle off the aftercare instructions for the seventh time in your life. You know you will not follow any of these directions. You have never been all that good at following anybody's instructions, even if it's for your own good.

You stop at Chipotle on the way home to peel off the bandage. This part no longer phases you. The tape used to drive you to swearing, but now you just silently remove the tape and ball it up into the trash. You move on with your day. This is becoming routine for you. You will spend fifteen minutes in the Chipotle bathroom trying to get a decent picture of your new ink. This is more difficult than you had originally assumed because it is, after all, on your back. You will take at least fifteen pictures of the floor, the mole on your shoulder blade and your ass before you get a decent snapshot of your ink. You will upload this picture to Facebook with a caption that reads "Drawn by me, ink by T'ill Death."

Your mother will call you tomorrow, her voice outraged and weepy over the long distance phone call. You will try to console her, reassuring her that what you have done is only skin deep. She will respond by saying, "With a tattoo like that, you can't expect me to believe that you're not going to wind up pregnant." The world that raised your mother didn't allow women to outrun their stereotypes. She does not believe you will be able to outrun yours. You have every intention of doing what you do best: proving her wrong.

But for today your driver's seat is adjusted to lay all the way back, keeping the cushion from interfering with your ink. You wonder what other cars must think when they look over to see you with no backrest. Holding your own body up for the two hour ride makes you too aware of every bone in your back. You think of scoliosis, you think ab workout, you think hunchback. You think home is farther away than it seemed this morning.

When you walk into your apartment, you are bone sore tired. There is a pair of beheaded earbuds strewn across the kitchen floor. The headphones belong to your roommate's boyfriend. You will find out later that they are the first casualty of his fight with her that afternoon. Your roommate's boyfriend has moved all his belongings into the living room. He is considering moving out here. Your living room is not big enough for this. The living room is not far enough away from her room for this. You hear the angry murmurs of your roommate and this boyfriend like a poltergeist through the walls. Arguing couples have always felt too much like home.

You go pee. You realize that the bathtub is brimming with water clouded by soap scum. Your other roommate has clogged the drain with her unbrushed hair. You begin frantically scooping water from the tub with a lobster pot and dumping it over the railing of your fire escape. You don't want to give your roommate and her boyfriend another reason to fight. Arguing couples remind you of your parents in all the wrong ways.

You smother your Chipotle burrito in sriracha until it looks almost bloody, a small bleeding cadaver on a plate. Your knife clinks awkwardly against the silence of your kitchen. You scrape ¾ of the burrito into the trash. You think about how the rest of the night will play out if you stay here. Your spine is throbbing like a toothache. First the boyfriend would emerge from the room at the far end of the hall, explain his side of the story. Then eventually your roommate would storm into the kitchen and tell you something completely different. Both sides of this story are irrelevant though because you know she is just being pissy because the pharmacy is late on her meds this week. It has nothing to do with her boyfriend, and it definitely has nothing to do with you. You don't get paid to be a couples' therapist.

You can't stay, but you don't know where to run to either. Your apartment is a war zone and you just want to make it through the day without stepping on a landmine. You take a double shot of vodka. You open Facebook messenger. At least a dozen profile pictures of campus boys appear at the click of a button. All beg for you, beautiful, all dripping cheesy pick up lines and questions of "what's up?" as if they actually cared. With a face like yours, you never have to be alone, but you always find yourself lonely just the same. You sing out "eeeenie meeenie miney mo…" and find a place to go.

The boy that opens the dorm building door is not as bad as you were expecting. His face is too narrow, pinched into some kind of rat smirk. His name is Rich. He is ok enough, but too ugly to fall in love with. This is all you ever look for in a man. Not ugliness, per se, just someone who is flawed enough that you will not be too devastated when they inevitably leave or lose interest. You have stopped believing that these things won't happen; you have started preparing for them instead. The boy has cold eyes, calculating and cynical. He'll always be more interested in your tattoos and your ass than with your face and the words that come out of it.

You follow him up a stairwell that you remember well from Freshman year, when you and one of your friends would wander through the halls on a Saturday night as drunk as you would ever be. You had never really been looking for a place to go as much as you were just looking to be seen. You didn't realize then that reputations set like cement around your feet. You didn't realize until you woke years later to find yourself sinking in an ocean you no longer wanted to swim in. But being in a dorm now, makes you feel younger, takes you back to when life had little consequence and any problem you had disappeared when you went home for break.

Rich's dorm room looks like every other boy's you have ever been in: very little decoration, very much clutter, a graveyard of bottles glinting on the windowsill so that everyone walking by on the sidewalk can admire this testament to delinquency.

You warn him that your tramp stamp is fresh. He smiles like you've told him a dirty secret and grinds your back harder into his mattress. The bedspread will be dotted with blood in the morning, like strange freckles on an unfamiliar face. He does not understand that the moth on your back is an open wound. He will never understand that you are an open wound.

You wake up the next morning. You watch three episodes of "Weeds" with your face pressed into his pillow. The boy smells like bad axe spray and bong water. You smell like knock-off Chanel and blood. He traces the burnt red outline of your tattooed wings with a too long finger.

"This tattoo suits you," he will tell you. You want to snap at him. You want to tell him, *bitch, you do not even know me*. But you don't waste your breath anymore on people that will be gone tomorrow. You let the temporary believe what they will, each stranger carrying away a different version of you, like ants stealing crumbs from a picnic.

You make up an excuse about having to go home to put lotion on your tat. You don't want the wings to start peeling.

The truth is you've run out of words, out of stamina. You're getting bored with being horizontal. He doesn't quite believe you, but he kisses you hard, teeth barred and lets you go. You don't expect to see him again.

You walk home alone. You, with mid drift hiked high, butt length hair twisted into a bedroom knot, a smoky eye look drifting somewhere down your cheek. Middle aged women out for a power walk, elderly couples out for Sunday strolls eye your four inch heels, your red rimmed ink with scorn, disapproval. They don't understand; they have homes already. They have people to walk with. You don't know how to live as they live. You are some kind of lunar moth, mouthless and finite, just looking for the light.

A Pretty Woman's Field Guide to Poisonous Plants

Belladonna: with a name meaning "pretty woman," this poison's effects are anything but beautiful. This plant is notorious in nature for being a devil in disguise. A warning that things are hardly ever as they appear.

"That's it! I'm gonna go punch him in the face!" Shane says, getting high off my heartbreak's second hand smoke. Her face is about as red as her hair. Shane, me and whatever guy Shane dragged out of the Spring Fling college dance are standing in the student center lobby catching air. I feel like I'm suffocating. I'm overstimulated on bad rap and a tequila buzz. I am doing my best not to clap my hands over my ears, to start crying like good little drunk girls do. I am trying desperately to get an image of my almost-boyfriend, Rich, dancing with some other girl, out of my brain. He's just a string bean, I tell myself, suppressing the fact that suspiciously skinny has always been my type. He's got a rat face, pinched and cruel looking. I'm beating him up in my mind the way Shane wants to beat him up in person. Shane's guy is holding her hand, holding her back from running into the fray to kick Rich's ass. It's for the boy's own interest though; he will not be getting laid tonight if Shane gets arrested for decking Rich.

"I would rather you didn't hit him," I tell her. "Let's just go. I knew it was gonna happen, and I'm fine with that, but I don't need to watch it happen."

Shane shrugs, jumping onto the back of her boy toy, piggy back style as we make our way to the exit. I think the boy's name is Nathan, but I can't remember between the bass and the tequila. I have a hard time keeping my own name straight on nights like these, let alone anyone else's.

Nathan's not bad looking, but over toned, with muscles popping out at the edges like the loose stuffing of a teddy bear. He's the type of guy that actually would say, "Do you even lift bro?" But that's Shane's type anyways: gym rats.

It's a short walk home to my apartment through the commuter parking lot, but it feels like eternity. My fingers are itching for a cigarette, anything to hold on to, to settle their shaking. I like to act like shit don't phase me, but sometimes trying to keep it all together is like sitting in a burning house and trying to ignore the smoke. *Just make it through this parking lot without sobbing and we'll be ok, Liza,* I think to myself. I'm staring up at the sky, keeping the tears in their ducts through gravity. A full moon stares back at me, denying my right for any star to wish on, no matter how much I need it. I walk ahead, impatient to get out of these heels, get out of these too tight shorts that Nathan's eyes are glued to. I am through with being on display for the night.

"What'd you think of the girls making out in there?" Nathan asks, because it's been silent, oppressively, crushingly silent up until this point, with nothing to be heard but the scrape of our feet on the concrete. There had been a gaggle of girls at the dance, in bikini tops and heels, drunk and clinging, arms catching arms like tree branches in a hurricane. Lip glossed and tequila tinted lips locking, biting. It's a show, for the boys, for attention. There is no love there.

"Me and Liza kiss girls too!" Shane announces proudly from Nathan's back. "It's kinda our thing."

Nathan's bulldog face lights up with a smirk.

"Oh, really?" he asks. He's just won the lottery, walking two drunk, bi girls home. He's counting up his chips, and it appears to be amounting to a threesome. I gulp, terrified of the greed laid naked before me.

"But we don't kiss each other," I correct. Nathan looks as if I've just kicked him in the nads. "We know too much about each other. It'd complicate everything."

"Right," Shane agrees. I've saved our skins, but I don't want to admit that Shane is not my type, that I've seen what she's done to men and I'm not signing up for that kind of torture. She's a hilariously bitchy friend, but no, too cruel for anything else. Shane has a habit of eating people alive.

We reach the bottom of my fire escape porch, and I plow through the rose bush that is attempting to eat the railing. Thorns trail across my bare arms like tiny hungry sets of teeth.

"Good night guys," I shout behind me. "Don't do anything I wouldn't do."

"Wait!" Shane whines. "I have to grab my phone!"

I'm not sure I want Nathan in my house. I don't hold the branches back for them, they can come in, but I'm not going to make their path any easier. Shane pulls Nathan up the fire escape and through the door and into the living room. Nathan plops down on our ice cream stain splattered futon like he lives here. Shane yanks her phone from the wall, scrolling through her screen while she drapes her legs across Nathan's lap. I do what I usually do when I'm unsure of what to do with my hands; I fix us drinks. Blueberry vodka and lemonade.

"This doesn't have roofies in it, right?" Nathan asks when I hand him a mason jar. I laugh dryly because I'm trying to take it as a joke, because I don't have the energy to explain that it's not. I change the subject.

"Adam's girlfriend was there alone..." I think aloud. Adam's girlfriend had been dancing by herself, but no, not smiling, she never seemed to be happy. I wanted to shake her; you have everything that I want! Be happy dammit! But I'm also terrified she'll kill me in my sleep, so I keep my distance. "Homewrecker," she had called me this winter, as if it were my name when she found my texts on Adam's phone. As if any of us in college really could call any place "home" yet. It was months ago, a wound scabbing over. But still my fingers itched to rip it open again. "Maybe I should be trying to hit Adam up tonight instead of worrying about the Rich thing...."

Shane looks like she did outside the dance, like she's ready to smack some sense into somebody.

"I will honestly have to kill you myself if you go running back to Adam again," Shane shrieks. Shane knows the history too well. Whenever my life is out of control, I run to him. Adam doesn't ask me questions about what's wrong or where I've been, we just pick up where we left off, as if he'd never left at all. "You are not going to ruin things with Rich because of that asshole."

The second Rich looped his arms around another girl's waist, things were ruined. It had nothing to do with me. I don't have the energy to explain this to Shane. There is nothing I could do to remedy this, nothing I can do that would poison it further either. Our relationship is dying, and the best I can do is pretend I don't care. The person who wins any break up is the one who leaves with the most blood on their hands. I will be that victor.

My fingers are on my phone and I'm texting Adam, breaking our four months of silence like a vow of chastity.

***

Growing nearly five feet tall, the Belladonna flower is a welcoming shade of pink, with petals stretched out like open arms. She's a beauty, an eye catcher for certain, and there's where her danger lies. No one could believe that something so beautiful could be so evil, until it's too late.

***

An hour later, Shane's home asleep. Nathan has wriggled his way into my bed. I'm pacing a hole in the floor of my room, waiting on two other guys: Adam to text me he's coming over and Rich to text me and tell me to come over to his dorm. Nathan, this six foot of idiot under my covers is a human roadblock to both plans and I wish he'd leave. Or die, whichever works. He came back for his phone and said that he would stay for a drink, but clearly he was thirsty for something other than vodka.

For the first time in my life, I am saying no. I can't pull another person into this burning building that I call my body. I should be condemned, but still I stand, with shiny windows and an open door.

"I just can't!" I say for what seems like the fifth time since Nathan got there. My fingers are woven through my hair, gently threatening to tear it from my skull if the situation calls for it. I'm sitting on my floor, because with Nathan sitting in it, my bed is a foreign country. I'm shirtless and I don't remember why.

"Tease," Nathan says. It's something I've never been called before. *Whore*, yes. *Slut*, yes, but I always go too far to be just *tease*. I don't tease, I bully, I invoke emotional and physical trauma. I hit and run. My choices are fatal, not irritating. A bullet wound and never a rash. I thought the word *tease* would make me feel powerful, as if I were in control of my own destiny, as if the thing I was protecting was worth something. But instead the letters sit in my throat like a dry heave, a sickness with nothing to show for it.

"You don't understand," I clamor. "I'm caught between a new flame and an old burn, a new possibility or the love of my life." Nathan laughs at my sentiments. Only a girl would phrase it this way. I do not usually speak like a girl. Admitting that I have feelings is new territory for me to tread, and I'm terrified of falling through the ice.

"Between the string bean and the drug addict," Nathan summarizes all he's heard about my guys in a simple sentence. I want to ask Nathan why he thinks he is any different. A twenty- four-year-old at a college dance prowling for jailbait. A dude that thinks he's gonna hit me up with a one night stand after dancing with my friend all night. Nathan is no better than Rich, than Adam. If anything he is worse.

"You don't understand. We have history," I plead, but I know I am only speaking on behalf of Adam. My debate sided with him the moment he entered the equation, it always did. Nathan pulls me back to the bed and tries to kiss me; I don't kiss back.

"We could make history," he whines. I laugh. No, it's not a laugh, it's the cackle of a child- eating witch. I cover my mouth, embarrassed at my cruelty to a man who is only going after a pretty girl. He does not realize that he is bargaining for a monster. But pick up lines? Come on.

"Please get off of me," I demand. Nathan surrenders, and I sit back on the floor, pulling on my Hooters tank top.

Nathan looks hurt. He's trying not to look at me, examining my artwork thumbtacked across the walls because I can't stand blank space anymore than I can stand silence. The paintings are near pornographic images of red girls wrapped around blue boys. The girls are vines, using the bodies of the boys for support. The girls cannot stand on their own.

"Ya know, I just thought we could be like those people in your paintings," Nathan says.

"They are not people," I correct. "It is one boy and one girl, the same every time."

"That's not how I heard the story," he's calling me on my bullshit and it stings, because as much as I'd like it to, life rarely imitates art. "How can you be in love with two people at once?"

"Well, you're still in love with the first person, but the universe won't let you be together, so you still love him, but you can't have him. But hey, this other guy will do for now while you're waiting. You could practice with this guy for a while," I explain. I wince. How would Rich take it if he knew he was only *practice?* I could never *love* Rich, but I did love being loved by him; it gave me something to do with my hands.

"But once you commit to one person, that's it. If you were truly in love with the first person, then you wouldn't have fallen for the second," Nathan says. The poor sap is quoting Johnny Depp and he doesn't even know it. But maybe he's right? Maybe I do not love, could not love anyone but Adam.

Adam is a nicotine addiction to me. I can make up any excuse I want; I just need something to do with my hands; I just need something to take the edge off. I only do this when I'm drunk. But anyone can see it in the shaking of my fingers, in the way I say his name. I am hopelessly addicted, and though I carry this love around with me like a cancer in my chest, I cannot seem to quit for the life of me even though it is slowly killing me. I don't have the energy or the willpower to fall for anyone new.

I'm frustrated, angry. Nathan's making me think, and I survive by sweeping things under the carpet.

"Adam has a girlfriend now," I admit, trying to explain. I have never heard how stupid this sounds outside of my own mind. I love Adam, but could never put my finger on why. It doesn't matter; this stranger has no capacity to comprehend fate. He is too busy quoting Facebook inspirational memes to try to get my shirt back off.

"It's about who wants to know how your 3pm was, not about who wants you at 3am," Nathan quotes and the words echo my mother's advice. I want to scream, but I know I can't. What will this look like? A strange man playing Buddha in boxers in my bed. "Otherwise they'll use you to the bone and then there'll be nothing left. You'll have sold your soul for nothing."

"Souls don't exist," I say. It still feels like blasphemy dripping off my Catholic tongue. It's what I've come to believe because it is too tragic a consideration to process that I had a soul once and lost it out of boredom.

"Oh, really?" Nathan asks, an eyebrow cocked. "If souls didn't exist, then you'd be on top of me right now." I wince because I can picture it behind my eyelids and I don't like what I see.

"I think underneath whatever you're going through, you're probably a really nice person," Nathan tells me.

"No," I say, shaking my head as fervently as I did when I was trying to get him to stop kissing me. "No, I'm really not."

***

Belladonna takes its namesake from the pretty women of old Italy. They would use Belladonna extract as eye drops to dilate their pupils and make them appear more seductive with their enhanced Bambi eyes. The "prettier" the women got, the closer to blindness they became.

***

Nathan walked me to Rich's dorm building through the pitch black. The moon had gone behind a cloud and I couldn't see a foot in front of my face.

"You're beautiful," Nathan said at the door, even though the view of my face was gloomy at best. "Have a nice life." He kissed me on the forehead and walked away. I watched the night swallow him whole.

"Come back," the words knocked at the back of my teeth, but I wouldn't let them out. Nathan had helped me see things clearly, and now with him gone I felt my blindness closing back in around me. I pressed my forehead against the glass of the door and watched my reflection breathe fog until I could no longer make out my bambi eyes staring back at me. Rich swung the door open and I fell into his too-thin arms, with his cold eyes staring down at me from his too-narrow face. I suppress the voice in my head that is commenting on how ugly our babies would be.

In the hour since then, me and Rich have fucked in the bathroom, in the shower, with most of our clothes still on. He's still drunk and I am too, but not as much as I would like to be. He put his fist over my mouth, because we both knew that I could never keep quiet. I bit at his fingers, playfully, trying to get free. I laughed in spite of myself. Our lips locked and it tasted like Rolling Rock and watermelon gum. It wasn't great and it was short lived, but an adventure and an apology. This was a moment that will be very "us" when "us" is no longer a thing.

We've fucked in his dorm bed, his roommate in the next bed over.

"He's asleep, it's ok," Rich assures me, but I can still hear the rustling

61

of covers and the rhythmic glide of skin against skin. I am not stupid and his roommate is not asleep. I am a porn star putting on a live performance. When Rich bites my neck, all I can think about is why am I not getting paid?

"It's time for bed," Rich says when he's through with me, because he doesn't know what else to do with me. I drape his arm across me like a seatbelt because I like this part about him, this illusion that if I crash, he will keep me safe. Should I forgive him? I have committed so much worse tonight than he had even come close to doing. My anger has cooled to nothing but a sad understanding. After all, he called me home at the end of the night, he chose me in the end. But it is not enough. He will never be enough.

"I might have to leave," I admit. "My roommate is, like, puking." It's a lie. Truth is, I'm waiting for Adam to text me back, waiting to run back to him because after all this time, I still look forward to his visits like the second coming; the end of the world and possibly the only thing that makes it worth existing at all.

Rich buys it, either because he is too drunk to care or he honestly doesn't give a shit either way. Or is it because he trusts me? No, I cannot bear to think that now. I'm already in too deep to think that now. I don't belong to him. He made that clear today. I don't give a fuck anyways. I'm cradling my phone in my hand like a baby bird. The heart of our embrace is an impending betrayal and like any good time bomb I'm waiting for it to go off and break us in two.

***

Used occasionally to treat insomnia, Belladonna walks a fine line between sweet dreams and death. One drop too many and you'll never have trouble sleeping again. Also called nightshade, Belladonna has a way of turning the day into night.

***

It's 4:30 and I don't know if it's night or morning. I'm racing home in kitty heels, a block ahead of Adam so that he'll never know that I have spent my time waiting for him twiddling someone else's dick and not twiddling my thumbs. My soul is a shade of black, the tint of the heavens before people are supposed to be up in the morning. The sky is breaking like an eggshell, cracking into a morning that will be too optimistic for me to stomach. I have a way of living every moment candy coated in doom. My love for Adam is tragic. It will not go like the song says; no love, marriage, or fucking baby carriages. We will not make it out of these affairs alive. I fear I cannot make it through the night. I only exist at night. I would shoot down every lark in the branches lest their morning song awake the dawn.

"Baby, what are you doing with your life?" I ask a fading moon, but the man in it has no answers for me.

***

Belladonna has occasionally been used recreationally. It is known to be a psychoactive aphrodisiac and to induce hallucinations. This is rare due to the likely possibility of accidental overdose. Those who survive report notoriously bad trips that they never wish to repeat.

Belladonna trips are marked by hellish, threatening and demonic images. Some would argue the dangers are outweighed by a heightened sense of awareness and the lucid dreaming the pretty woman drags along with her. Being on Belladonna feels a lot like being in love, it feels a lot like hell on earth.

***

I barely recognize Adam when he shows up on my fire escape. I want to tell him stories about a lost little party girl and the boy who let her borrow his shoes because she was too drunk to walk home in heels. A fairy tale about a vodka punch Cinderella in vans slippers. But we are not those people anymore. Our once upon a time was too long ago for it to matter anymore.

"S'up?" I say to the stranger who sticks his cigarette-rolled tongue down my throat, choking me with the taste of history.

"S'up," he echoes. He wears glasses now, he puts them in my jewelry box for safe keeping. He's skinnier now, like his skeleton has sensed the end is near and wants out before the whole building goes down. It's trying to edge its way out of his doomed skin anyway it can. My skin and bones in shining armor coming to my rescue once again, no questions, no explanation needed. I want nothing more than to be buried in his grave dirt eyes.

There is a hunger here. We rip at each other's throats like caged pit bulls, trained to kill. I taste blood when I kiss him, biting his lip. I can no longer tell if it's my blood or his that has been spilt at this altar and perhaps it makes no difference anymore. I am carving canyons in his back, sowing tiny rows with my fingernails to plant a vengeance in his girlfriend. *I was here, bitch!* I'm carving my initials across his skin like it's the bark of a tree, because this is what lovers do. Perhaps we will be lovers again but, if I know one thing for certain, it's that nothing is ever certain.

I know now the ecstasy that I could not explain to my stranger earlier tonight. You cannot explain religion to a non-believer. Adam's saying my name like a psalm, a safe word that's gonna deliver him. This is as close to heaven as two sinners are ever gonna get. His hand's in a fist around my neck, biting shoulders, tendons, *I'll eat you up I love you so baby, if only you'd give me the time.*

I can't breathe, but I don't live off oxygen anymore. I'm filling my lungs with sips from his lips. I read once that kissing builds bonds, and that's why prostitutes don't do it. If I can just keep my mouth there, maybe he will keep me forever. I'm barely moving my lips from his, desperate, like I'm trying to resuscitate a corpse, bring us back to life. If I keep kissing, will he stay with me? If I kiss till my mouth is dry and I can no longer speak my own name, will he let me fall asleep in his arms? Will he call out my name always, like the dirtiest curse he knows and the strongest act of contrition?

For the first time in all our years of fuckery, Adam stays the night. He is too big for my bed, his six foot limbs dangling off the sides of the mattress at weird angles that remind me of roadkill. He's snoring within seconds. There is no room for me by his side, but I am used to this by now. I lay a blanket out on the floor and try to get some sleep.

It's seven in the morning. Shane will be waking up soon, waiting for a text from Nathan that will never show up. Rich will be waking up alone soon, still believing I was mopping up vomit somewhere across town. I lied to him. I cheated. We will never be the same. Whatever hope we had for a mutual future has been doused. I have strangled our relationship cold with my bare hands. Adam's girlfriend will be waking up alone soon, in tears, because she knows exactly where he went. I'm losing track of how many ways I've broken her heart. I'm tossing and turning over all the poison seeping from the work of my hands into everyone else's life. I did it for love, I defend to myself. But even I know that that's just putting a pretty name on an ugly thing.

***

If a dose of Belladonna is left untreated, it will eventually result in death. Only 7% of victims have been known to survive. If you do not heed the warning, the Belladonna may be the last thing you ever see.

How to Be Found

It is your twenty-first birthday and you wake up alone. Everyone else has work today. You do not mind. You have plans, like getting day drunk alone. You go to Hannaford's in your pjs like a kid on Christmas morning. You cry tears of joy in the liquor aisle. You collect the ingredients for a "drunken girl scout" shot; Malibu rum, caramel vodka, chocolate syrup. You have this expectation that you will make fancy drinks now that you can pick out your own alcohol, complicated recipes from Pinterest that suburban housewives make for their fellow soccer mom friends. This will never be the case. You are not suburban housewife material. You are and always have been a straight from the bottle type of mess.

You mix orange juice and Malibu in a mason jar that once held home-canned pickles and beets preserved for you with love by your mother. You think about all the things her hands have ever made. The only thing you've ever pickled is your liver.

You sneak the jar into the movie theater. You watch *Alice in Wonderland: through the looking glass* twice because you missed the transition from one showing to the next. You think about Alice, how her entire book was originally a love letter written to an underage girl from her math teacher. You think about how great it would be for someone to love you enough to write a book in your honor. You do not realize how warped and lonely this reaction is.

No one comes looking for you to kick you out, to check your ticket.

You are the only person in this movie theater. You think about how beautiful the quiet is, how easy. You think about how soft the velvet dark of muffled lights is, softer than any bed you've ever shared. You think of how artificial butter could easily become your favorite perfume, if you could just stay here. If it's any consolation, you don't have to talk to anybody here. Escapism, they call it. You forgot to notice the moment when your life became nothing more than a series of fire exits.

You get a text from Rich, your phone vibrating intrusively into the dusky black of the theater. *Happy Birthday,* he says. He is out of town working (you don't know what his job is and you don't ask), but when he gets back he promises to take you to dinner. You still believe in the crossed finger promises of false prophets. You are so over the moon about the possibility of being taken on an actual date that you overlook the fact that you will be spending your birthday night alone.

You go home. You order a jalapeno calzone for dinner that you will not eat. Your eyes are always bigger than your stomach. You wait for your friends to come back from work. You write about and wait for people who will be strangers to you in a year's time.

Each of your roommates trickles back through the door. Mercy gets back from lifeguarding, hair wreaking of chlorine and begging a shower. Robbie, a vegan, gets back from his shift at McDonald's, dressed in a cheap polo shirt and irony. Shane gets back from emptying bedpans at the nursing home all day. She is already showered and winged eyeliner ready. Shane always looks like she's keeping a secret, always looks like she's in trouble. She has a bad habit of making resting bitch face look sexy.

Robbie and Mercy are getting ready, so you pour Shane a shot, hoping to slake the pissed off look she's got on her face. You pour yourself a shot, you link arms and sling them back together. She asks you questions you cannot answer about your love life.

"What's with Adam lately?" she asks.

"He's been around," you shrug. You have a habit of minimizing everything, terrified of jinxing what could be with the trip wire of your words.

"So you broke it off with Rich, then?" she asks, because for any other person this would be a logical assumption. You pull out the text from him from earlier that day as if it's an engagement ring. She cocks an eyebrow, always amused at the holes you dig for yourself.

"You gotta choose," she says, because this would be the sane thing to do, this would be the humane thing to do. You just shrug. You know that you don't *gotta* do anything.

You walk to the bar together. The bouncer, a burly man with sleeve tattoos, will spend more time looking at your cleavage than at your ID. You will kick yourself, because you know now that you probably could've gotten in whenever you wanted to, regardless of your age. School is out, so the place is dead, a gaggle of townie bar flies congregate around the bar and little else. The jukebox is playing something you danced to in middle school. In the glimmer of the neon, all you can think to ask yourself is: *This? This is what you have been waiting for all these years?*

Shane will complain to you all night about her overprotective boyfriend. Mercy will drink too much for her distance runner frame. Robbie will spend much of the night making sure that Mercy does not drop her golden hair into the toilet bowl, because that's what true love is. You order two grateful deads. You puke in a graffiti covered bathroom stall. You hold your own hair back. You rinse out your mouth in the sink. You rally. You walk out and pretend nothing happened. You are red eyed and foul mouthed. No one asks if you are ok.

You walk to the next bar, the one that Adam works at. It is unusually hot for May, and your feet are sloshy sweaty in your metal studded heels. Your long blond hair is getting caught in your armpits, sticky and clinging. Shane and you clasp hands, swinging them back as though you are on a field trip, half mocking the way Mercy melts into Robbie, as you walk.

"I take back what I said," Shane says

"About what?" you ask, because you can't follow your own train of thought right now, let alone her's.

"You don't have to choose anybody," she says. "You're so lucky, you're so free."

You had never thought about it this way before. This thing that she called *free* always just felt more like nobody giving a damn about you. This thing came at a higher price than she was giving it credit for.

"I do think that you and Adam's children would be beautiful though," she says. "Your baby girl would never have to buy her own drinks, that's for sure."

You don't know what to do with this comment. You don't know if it's premonition, compliment or bullshit. But you are saved by the sudden scream of a truck wailing on it's horn behind you. You shriek in spite of yourself. You are jumpy to a fault, and know enough by now to be afraid of men in trucks at night. In the early summer heat, a chill goes up your spine. There is tequila trying to persuade its way up the back of your throat but it's argument is one you refuse to listen to.

The man behind the steering wheel, a square jawed and stern faced townie waves at Shane, who drops your hand and waves back. Something clicks into place in your mind. This is the boyfriend you've heard so many complaints about. He loops the truck into the parking lot of the bar. He is fearful of "girls' nights" going too late, tracks Shane's movements as if she is on probation. He has come to collect his inmate.

Shane runs around to the passenger side, spitting goodbyes and apologies back at you as she goes. You watch the only thing standing between you and third wheeling disappear around the bed of the truck. Shane is out of earshot, the boyfriend leans his head out the driver's side window.

He extends his hand out to you, for you to shake. "Hi, I'm Emmett," he says. "and you must be beautiful."

You wince. You do not believe it when people tell you this anymore.

In the booth inside the bar, Mercy will lean her tired skull against Robbie's boyish shoulder. Your bleach blonde head has nobody to lean on and this is a problem for you. Your mind is sometimes too heavy a thing for you to hold up on your own. You text Adam, ask him when he is getting off work. He promises to meet you after. He will be too drunk to remember by the time after work rolls around. But for now you are stupid and half-hearted hopeful.

There are baseball games flitting by on the twin TVs on the wall. A man sitting on a bar stool keeps asking you personal questions with a slurred mouth: *name? age? where do you live, sweetie?* You make up answers for each inquiry: *Bathsheba, 69, California.* Mercy is growing queasy and tired of your antics. Her patience is pulled tighter than the tendons on her too skinny neck. She says you can stay, but she's going home. Robbie looks like a man tied to two different horses. You concede to just follow them back. There is nothing here for you anyway.

You walk home, see that the apartment door has been left open. Mercy's cat is gone. You wander the neighborhood, calling for a cat you had never really wanted in your apartment to begin with. You search through trailer park potholed roads and past rows of party houses, their lights dimmed in the early hours of the morning. No cat. The man in the moon glares down at you, too bright and judging. He knows exactly where the cat is from his perch in the sky. He knows the location of every lost thing. But he's not gonna tell you shit. You do what you do best, you give up.

You try to fall asleep to the sound of Mercy puking in the next room over. You try to fall asleep with your phone on your chest like an EKG machine, so that if Adam texts you, you won't miss him entirely. If it vibrates, it will wake you, bring you back to life. You no longer believe in him enough to stay awake for him. You think about Sleeping Beauty, lying in wait to be awakened by her prince, because some drunk little lost girl part of you always wants to believe there is something fairy tale in this. Only sober you knows that your life is far from a bedtime story. You try to fall asleep in this bed that is too big for you alone, you are drowning in covers, swimming so deep in the sheets that you are afraid no one will ever find you.

You wake up to scratching on the front door. 4 am. Your birthday is over. You have no new text messages. Adam has forgotten you, forsaken you last night and you are not surprised. The cat has found its way home, dreamy eyed and hungry. You think of all the times you have stumbled back through that front door at a strange hour of the night, with just as little explanation. You pat the cat's head, say, "I know how it is."

You shut the door. Outside the window the sky is turning white at the edges, as if it's losing circulation. You can almost feel the pins and needles in the air. The birds are conversing way up in the trees. You feel as though they're gossiping about you. *Poor girl, how sad, waited up all night for a man who never came.* Morning is unhinging her jaws and you feel like you haven't slept a wink. Your eyes are bloodshot. You taste blood in your mouth, and it almost reminds you of the way he kisses. But you shake the thought away. You will be tired today, with nothing to show for it.

You know you should get some sleep, but you close your eyes and you see his face. You only drift off by imagining his body cupped around yours, the way it has never been in real life, the way that you want it to be. Someday, if not yesterday, if not today. One day. He is asleep across town, in some other girl's bed, not giving a damn about you. You are the only person tossing and turning over all the sins you've left uncommitted this night. People often ask you how you sleep at night, considering everything you've done, everything you've seen. You sleep mornings, you want to tell them, you sleep days. You have become some kinda nocturnal creature, all glowing eyes and fangs. A vampire, bloodthirsty, and going to bed this morning, still hungry, still empty, still cold as the grave that is your empty bed.

You go back to sleep thinking about how many people went looking for a cat that night, how no one ever bothered to look for you. About how often things find their way home, without being found, without help and without hope. Maybe you will too.

A Gambler's Guide to Getting Lucky

"You couldn't think of any other girls to bring with you?" Rich questions me when I walk into his apartment. There is no "hi" for me anymore. After two months of hook ups, he's no longer happy to see me. I am no longer enough. We've flip-flopped in this way. In the beginning, I saw nothing but a toothpick where a boy should be. Now he's my crutch, the only thing strong enough to keep me upright. The further I fall in love with anybody, the more they lean away. My eyes skim over everything about Rich that holds a flaw, to remind myself that I do not have to feel bad about his coldness. His face is narrow, pinched. He is too skinny, suspiciously so. He has begun growing out a mustache, a thin caterpillar frail but determined below his too pointed nose. I stare at him until I forget what I ever saw in him. I am out of his league in everything but confidence, of which I have none.

Rich is back for the night, from whatever traveling job he's accepted for the summer. I have not seen him in a week. The apartment is dimly lit, with music videos of mumble rappers playing over the big screen TV. This is a notorious party house, *Green House*, on the third floor of an apartment complex. The ceiling glows with pot leaves scrawled in glow-in-the-dark marker. The kitchen joins to the living room, with only a small divider running through it. I can see the faces of other college boys peering at me from beyond Rich's shoulders. I stand for a moment in the entryway, expecting something like a hello kiss. He turns away, fumbling back to the living room. I should've known better, but by now that is always the case.

The other boys crowded around the living room, however, are very happy to see me, little bombshell me in my lingerie top and kitty heels. I dress like a hired stripper, and I suppose this is what they see when they look at me. I do not know them, have never seen them before. Most of my life is spent with the person I am sleeping with and whatever strangers they drag through my world. A carousel of temporary people spinning around me while I stand still, going nowhere but around in a circle, making myself dizzy. The boys nudge Rich on the elbow, pat him on the back when they think I'm not looking, my head in the freezer retrieving Captain Morgan I was offered but not served.

"You didn't even take your shoes off?" Rich asks me from the living room between pipe puffs. I look down at my heels, self conscious now, the points of them leaving a trail of indents in the carpet floor, like the tracks of some hunted animal through the snow.

"I like my shoes... they're pretty," I say, but what I really mean is that I want to be always run ready, that I can never really make myself comfortable anywhere, anymore.

The boys gathered here, apparently, have a court date in the morning. We are celebrating their last night of freedom, by committing the same crime they got impounded for to begin with: getting wasted. The cops were called on the apartment for the last party, and now they're all going in for underage drinking, for possession. I hadn't been there, had ironically been safe with Adam in some other apartment, in some other bed. I call this luck, but I know it's only a matter of time before it is me waiting for a verdict. I am always near, but never in trouble. There's no way that the boys, that Rich, will get anything more than community service, but still we're drinking like the world is gonna end, and perhaps, maybe, it is.

I walk to the futon cautiously, this floor is hallowed ground, even though there are discarded weed nugs clinging to the toes of my heels. The apartment we're sitting in once belonged to a one night stand of mine that happened two more times than necessary. It was our

Sophomore party house. The guy who rented it, Carson, ruled over it like Jay Gatsby, throwing epic parties where students from all walks of life wandered in without invitation; they didn't need one. The night called you here. You may have begun somewhere else, but you always landed here. And maybe this is why I slept with Carson, a stout pirate looking guy, not conventionally attractive by any means. I didn't want to possess him. I wanted to *be* him, wanted to live this man's life where he could sit comfortably on his futon and watch the world light up and burn all around his feet. But the king had graduated. Everything I had known to be sure had disappeared, and yet, here I was two years later, still stuck in the same place I'd always been.

I realize that I have been spacing out, staring at the same Bob Marley poster for the past five minutes. Marley stares back from the wall, his kind and dopey face offset by a Rasta striped background. If I asked anyone in this room, I don't think they could even tell me what Rastafarianism is. I contemplate for a moment that any man that smiles like Marley must be able to treat a woman right, be her home and her adventure. I vow to find a man with a Marley smile while I sit in my current man's apartment. This is how temporary I have labeled my life with Rich. I am already contemplating his successor as he sits on the futon across from me, smoking a bowl. If he could read my mind at any given time, would he still call me clingy? I'm sucked up into that quiet tunnel vision I get when I drink too much, banging my fists against the inside of my own brain, trying to bully it into letting me out. But it won't budge.

"Your girl looks like she's about to fall asleep," the boy that looks like Shaggy from Scooby Doo says. Rich shrugs. I am not his girl, but I am his problem. Shaggy keeps crossing the living room to offer me things from twisted glass pipes that I need to ask him how to use. I take what he gives me like a child choking on bubble gum Benadryl. *It's for your own good honey, you'll feel better soon, doctor's orders.*

"Can you light this for me?" I bat my Bambi eyes at Shaggy, handing him back the lighter. "It's bad luck to light it on your own."

I've made this superstition up because what they've given me is nearly cashed and I can't get the angle right without burning my fingers. *She's a girl, she won't notice*, that's what they think. I've been around long enough to know how this game is played, and how to win. My question sounds like flirting. Everything I say sounds like flirting. I'm a pin-up with a heartbeat and I can't help it. I'm watching Rich out of the corner of my eye, waiting for a wince of jealousy, but there's nothing for me in his rat thin face, even with Shaggy's nose brushing up against mine.

Is it apathy? Or just the hazardous ingredients Rich has just consumed coming to a boil? I'm sick of looking for possession in all the wrong places. I light my own after this, watching my fingernails catch flame like the fingertips of a wrathful god. Let the bad fortune I had warned against come. I'm already shit outta luck.

***

To a young Dorothy Rothschild, it seemed that her family's luck had drowned alongside her distant cousin on the Titanic. Her mother was dead. Her stepmother was a nightmare. She wished on every eyelash, dandelion seed and birthday candle for her stepmother's demise. But when her hope proved true, all she could find were barbs of guilt jabbing where relief was supposed to have sprung. Dorothy had not expected Death to listen to the whims of a child, and now it was too late. Dorothy knew now to be careful what you wished for. Sometimes what you had thought you wanted was not so wonderful once you had gotten it, once the reality of the thing had settled its bones for a long stay. Her father died soon after, if you hadn't known him, you'd say of a broken heart. Dorothy knew better than that by now. Dorothy found herself young and breathtakingly alone in the world.

Dorothy would later say that she only ever looked for three things in a man: handsomeness, stupidity and ruthlessness. She found all those things in a soldier, Eddie Parker. There is nothing more heartbreaking than meeting the right person at the wrong time. There was a war coming, and Eddie would always be in the wrong line of work. Dorothy and Eddie spit in the eye of fate and married anyway. Eddie had to leave her. She followed him for a time, visiting bases in New Jersey, Georgia, but you can't follow a soldier everywhere; you cannot follow a man into battle, no matter how hard you try. Within her first year of marriage, Dorothy found herself an ocean away from her husband, alone once again. Such had always been her luck.

***

My mother always told me I was a lucky girl. The summer I was five-years-old, I came home one day to find a cage on the dining room table, a spare Snow White sheet from my bed hung about it's framework like it was playing Halloween ghost. Da, a man as large, jagged and sprawling as a mountain range paced the carpet in his cracked steel toe boots.

"What is it Daddy?" I asked, my fingers stubbed and sticky from the skin of fruit snacks I had eaten in the car reached up for the mystery where it sat on the table. Mama, all permed hair, hooked nose, beautiful glared at Daddy, he always had a bad habit of dragging stray things home with him.

Daddy pulled the sheet back with the flair of a magician. The first thing my young eyes fell upon was the cage. How intricate, how beautiful it stood in its captivity. The bars were arranged just so that the sherbert colored arms of them came together to form something resembling a Victorian house. Two birds, a flurry of margarita green, stop sign orange and piss yellow cowered together on the floor of the cage. Two birds of paradise so very far away from home.

"They're love birds," Daddy explained. "And they're all yours."

I poked a stubby finger through the bars of the cage, tried to talk sweet nonsense to the birds to make them less afraid of me. I wanted to see them fly.

"John, do you have any idea how long those things live for?" my mother protested, apprehensive about yet another mouth (or rather beak) to feed.

My father shrugged, raising his candy apple red suspenders up and down. I know now that the birds were meant to outlive me. Their lives often spanned the breadth of centuries. My father was trying to buy a lifetime for me. Unfortunately, that's not how it worked out.

***

Owen, the boy who looked like he was about to vomit, is now passed out on the couch. His bug eyes are shut, his sloping smile wavering in sleep. I won't be able to recognize this person tomorrow. I don't bother to keep track of the names and faces of the fleeting anymore. I will need that space in my brain for something more important, someday. Shaggy's gone home. Rich wants to go on a field trip. I want him to fuck me on the kitchen table, but we agree to do things his way.

The only other person left is his manager (of what job, I was never quite sure), a man with a thinning hairline and a porn stache that looks like he's old enough to be my father, regardless of how many times Rich assures me that he's our age. Manager talks my ear off from the porch out into the street. He speaks to me in little bite size pieces the way that men who admire me do. It makes me feel like Marilyn Monroe, as if they assume that my hair bleach soaked up all my brain cells along with it. But I don't really mind. I like when people underestimate me. I am not left responsible for the architectured disasters that befall my world.

The streets are near empty, too late on a dead town Wednesday summer night. I'm reminded of *The Notebook,* a movie that I'll never admit to watching. I'm reminded of how the two lovers laid in the middle of the road when night swallowed up their small town and the stoplight faded to a glowing yellow. I know that no one will ever lay in the road with me, but I'm flaunting all this empty pavement anyway, dodging on and off the sidewalk, tempting fate, trying my luck.

Rich talks to me the way that Manager does, as if I am younger than

I am, but his voice is getting threadbare, shredding like that of a nagging parent after months of coping with me.

"Leeza, I swear to God, if you go in the road one more time…." But I do continue to run in the road, drunken foot tumbling after drunken foot. I'm free. A truck takes our corner sharply, barreling down the potholed pavement too fast, and too loud. The headlights catch me like the midnight eyes of a predator, reflecting like coins in the dark. I offer out my chest and the sad little monster beating inside it. Here I am road, at your altar. Take me home. *Take me home country road,* like the lullaby my father used to sing to me in the car. The truck will see me, stop. I do not have a death wish, just a near death wish. I walk a tightrope with trouble, constantly trying to see how close I can get to the edge without falling in.

Rich has got me now by the strap of my purse, pulling me back onto the sidewalk, pulling me back to him. I am not getting away that easy. I got a child leash, when all I really wanted was a spanking.

"Leeza, where do you think you're going?" he pronounces my name wrong even now, but I let it slide. It sounds exotic on his lips. And it's nice to be someone else for a change, even if it is only all in the name.

We wander home barefoot. It rained earlier in the day and the pavement glints up at us like the starlight the sky is too cloudy to betray at the moment. Mud cakes up the tip of the stilettos in my hands. I worry absentmindedly about how I will scrub this stain out tomorrow. The town is quiet, a Wednesday in the college off season. No one is celebrating but us, and we hardly have a reason to either. I watch my shadow swaying on the sidewalk ahead of Rich's and Manager's. If someone was to look just at our shadows, what would they see? A family? A couple and a third wheel? All I can see is a girl running away from two men in the night. The damp in the air gets to me, and I shiver like I've seen something I shouldn't have.

Our mason jars we'd brought with us, now empty of their rum and coke, are ditched in the university bushes. Our hands have better things to do than pick up after ourselves. We climb up the porch steps, three floors of stairs to the fire escape outside of Rich's apartment. We sit out there, three stories up above the world, the apartment that raised me looming like a ghost in the back drop. Manager is feeding me glasses, filling the tank for an empty goal. I feel bad for Manager with his prematurely receding hairline and his dad bod. No pretty girl will ever want him. He will always be sliding drinks into the manicured hands of his friends' lovers. A bystander in love and in life.

Rich gives me nothing, sits on the cooler on the porch, scrutinizing me with his too-cold eyes. He is checking me out, after two hours of me being here, assessing the way my navel peeks out from beneath my crop top, the way my tan line plays at the hemline of my shorts. He is relearning that outside of my text messages, needlessly caring and annoying, I am still hot. He is remembering all the reasons he has kept me around despite my childish ventures and my cloying words.

"Aren't you drunk?" Rich asks me tripping over syllables with hope because he loves me when I'm wasted.

"Nah— you?" I say. Manager looks at me with admiration from where he is leaning against the porch railing.

"Damn girl…" Rich hiccups, reminding me of Snow White's Dopey, staring at me from his seat on the cooler. "Yeah I'm fucked up." I slurp more, so he doesn't come off as such a lightweight, but it's to no end. I don't really feel anything anymore.

Someone had wheeled their office chair out onto the porch. This is what I'm sitting on, twirling the seat around like a carousel, hoping maybe I'll tip over the railing. I'm dizzy from the spinning. Dizzy from the questions Manager is firing at me, which amount to more than Rich ever has bothered to ask.

"What are you going to school for?" Manager asks me.

"Elementary Education and creative writing," I say.

"So you like kids?" he asks, because people always ask me about the boring major.

"I do," I say and let it fall at that. What I want to say is that I'm beginning to realize that

I hate other people's children. I am learning that when I grow up, I want to be a mother, not a teacher. But this dream is not something to speak about when you're drunk and unloved on a Wednesday night. This is a sober, Sunday morning aspiration. This wish has no place between my teeth on this porch.

"A teacher, is that really what you wanna be?" he asks. I shake my head, because a million girls grow up to be teachers, and I want to be different. I have the delicious fact that I will never see this person again, so it will never matter what I tell him.

"I want to be a tattoo artist," I lie. "I already have like 7 tattoos."

"Wow!" he says, his eyes big. Having a lot of tattoos gives people ideas about you that are not necessarily true. They think suicide girl, they think pain fetish, they think stripper. I am the manic pixie dream girl of everyone's dreams; I am my favorite character in my own novel, and little else. "Are you gonna get a lot more tattoos, would you say?"

"Probably," I shrug.

I am intoxicated on attention. All Rich has ever asked me was "Can I fuck you?" To which I always tell him yes. Maybe this is just nature, for the ugly boys to care and the ones you're sleeping with to not to. Maybe there just isn't room for souls and sex to occupy the same skeleton.

We're stargazing because we're closer to the sky up here almost on the roof. If I stretched my hands out, I'm sure one of my nails could scrape the heavens, rip right through the seam of it. I consider doing this for a moment, tearing a hole through the celestial ceiling, sticking my head through and asking if I can come home. But I keep my hands locked at my sides, on the spinny chair. Tell myself that I am afraid of losing my balance, of falling. Truth is, I'm afraid that heaven will always be too far out of my reach.

"I can see the big dipper!" Rich exclaims, hyped, pointing at the sky above our heads. He is pointing at nothing but a random congregation of stars. This constellation is actually on the other side of the house and nowhere in our line of vision. I don't know what he's pointing at, but this is not it. But he doesn't like to be corrected, so I keep my mouth shut.

A shooting star spits across the sky. An ejaculation, a sign from a higher power we're not so sure of. I wish for things I'm not even sure I want, but things that would make life easier. I'm not asking for this to be love, I'm just asking for this to be it. Please let him be it, because I can't stomach the thought of any more.

"Did you make a wish?" Rich asks. I shrug as though I hadn't seen shit.

***

Dorothy wished for time to pass her by. She tried her best to keep busy. She got a writing job, a corner office stuffed to the brim with perfume and cut outs from mortuary magazines. Her boss would choke on her perfume, and wince at the clippings staring back at him from her walls, advertisements for embalming fluid and cadaver diagrams staring back at him with the flippancy of pin up girls, all bare and smiling. Dorothy was a play critic who had no experience acting in her own right. At least not yet. Later in life she'd have plenty of hours of practice, keeping a smile plastered to her porcelain doll face. She insulted the wrong person, lost her job. Got a new one at a different magazine, a better magazine. She did what most military spouses are so good at doing: she killed time. After a while, this gave life to career. Then celebrity, if not infamy.

The man she spent so much time waiting for was never to return. Eddie, or at least the Eddie she had known, the Eddie she was in love with, never came home.

Eddie had spent the war as an ambulance driver. A hair's width away from machine gun blasts and mustard gas. His vehicle had been hit once. He spent the next three days trapped underneath it, in a pit, his limbs ensnared with that of the dead and dying. It is ridiculous to expect a man to rise from the grave unchanged. No one ever really comes back from the dead, not really.

The uniformed man that showed up on Dorothy's doorstep one morning was a stranger. His body was familiar, he still wore the mouth that she had seen in her dreams all this time. But every ghost of a smile had evacuated. His eyes lie sullen and vacant, flat and placid in the throes of morphine addiction. Dorothy's man had come home to her, but neither Dorothy nor Eddie were the same people anymore. It was just her luck to have a good thing twist so absolutely rotten. She would have preferred it if Eddie had died, she caught herself thinking sometimes. In the privacy of her new office, she'd slap herself across the face for thinking such blasphemy. Surely there were thousands of war widows all across the country who would give anything to be as lucky as she. She had no right to complain.

In Eddie's absence, Dorothy had rose to something akin to stardom. She had found friends, a writers' society, a round table at the Algonquin hotel that had become nearly as infamous as that of King Arthur. The people around this table were brilliant, they were mean, they were above all, funny. She was their princess. They could never get over such ugly words coming from the baby doll lips of such a pretty face. *If you lead a whore to culture*, so on and so forth.

She wanted so desperately to share her new world with Eddie, had dragged him to the round table, once, twice, three times. But Eddie just sat there, awkwardly, in a morphine haze. Eddie bored her new friends and they bored him. She simply couldn't make him see her new world the way she saw it. She became angry, lost, in her married life. She had liked it better when Eddie was out of reach. She began to do what she did when she felt her confidence falter; she sharpened her tongue and went off to battle. She spun a series of "bumbling Eddie" stories that she spat all over the round table for all to hear. If she cut Eddie to pieces, if she made him sound unworthy, then losing him was really no loss at all.

At least that's what she told herself. After a year or so, the couple separated. They would never live together as a married pair again in their lifetimes.

Dorothy became a wreck, what would become a constant state for her for the rest of her days. She had affairs with men who were themselves in "all degrees of marriage." Despite her best advice and efforts, she fell hopelessly and irredeemably in love. That was just her luck.

***

I named the birds Annica and Phillip because I had this eerie habit of bestowing person names on all my pets, overly formal and ill-fitting, as if they had once been something or someone else. I watched the pair of them as they went about their lives within the see-through walls of their Victorian cage. Love birds, Daddy had called them. My five year old mind wondered if they really could teach me anything about love and all that it was.

Annica was the escape artist of the pair, always tugging with her stop sign beak at the guillotine style doors that allowed me to refill their bird seed or water. Mama wrapped bits of pink pipe cleaner around the bars of the doors, securing them fast and barring Annica's exit.

"You don't want her to get out," Mama would explain. "She could end up outside in the snow, and then where would we be?"

I pressed my peanut butter and jelly smeared face against the glass of the kitchen window, watching snowflakes descend like tiny parachutes across the hillside of our yard, impossibly small soldiers evacuating a heaven that was surely in for a crash landing. I wondered at how Annica had come to land in a place that could be so hostile to her. I wondered about how freedom could sometimes equal death. When I pulled my mouth back from the glass, a jelly smeared echo of my mouth stared back at me, like the kiss of some small ghost.

Sometimes Annica and Phillip would make an egg, a bone white pebble, as smooth and promising as a Cadbury Easter candy strewn on the floor of their cage. There was nothing in the cage that Annica could use to make a nest, no small scrap of nature with which she could make a cradle for her baby. The lives of my love birds were clinical, metallic, no environment in which to raise a child. Annica would roll the egg into the corner and try her best to forget it. She would perch her little dinosaur feet up on the bar before her mirror and stare at her reflection for hours, as if this small shred of glass were a window, as if it offered her a view of a world far from here.

Phillip would eventually find the egg, chip at the skin of it until I'd look up to find his stop sign beak dotted with the white of it, shards of enamel clinging to his mouth with the desperation of a broken tooth. Phillip had no interest in Annica loving anything but him.

"Bad, bad birdie," I'd jeer at him with a child's sense of justice, shaking the cage a little as I did so to let him know I meant business.

"Don't yell at your bird," Mama would say, more for the sake of her morning sick headache than for the sake of Phillip. "He's just surviving the only way he knows how."

***

"Do you want me to go home?" I ask because Rich said that he was going to bed on the pull out couch next to Owen's sleeping head in the living room. It doesn't really seem like there is space for me here. Marley's face glares at me from the wall, his grin ghoulish now, in the half light. Everything about tonight is telling me that I'm not welcome here, and somehow I have not left yet. I don't really have any place I'd rather be.

"Stay if you want," he says and I do because I'm scared of the walk home, alone. It's three am and the witching hour has never been a friend of mine.

Manager goes to bed in the next room. The lights dim out. I close my eyes and try for sleep. The room is pitch black, tapestry blankets covering each window to seal the fumes and sights of the less than legal inside the walls of the apartment. I can feel Rich's thin hands playing piano with my ribcage. I have just recently watched *The Babadook* and

Rich's long fingers against my side in the dark are anything but reassuring. His hands drift lower, then back again, like I am clay on a wheel, molded under the pressure of his palms, in his image, to his liking. I should be, but I'm not expecting it when my shorts get peeled off inches away from Owen's sleeping face. My face glows red, embarrassment a fever in my cheeks, but it's too dark for him to see, so I don't have to wonder if he would even care.

"I'm too tired, but you can fuck me if you want," Rich says, like I'm the one that took off my own clothes. It seems like everyone's too tired to fuck lately. It's my job; they try to make it sound like my idea. I'm working my knees till they're sore lately, wearing holes in the skin that wraps around them like second hand fishnets.

I shake my head "no" into his collarbone, so he can see my refusal, even in the dark. "No" is a scary word for me. Every time I say "no" someone leaves. This time will be no different.

"Are you scared I'm going to hurt you?" he asks. I nod. But I'm not afraid of him hurting me in the way that he thinks. I'm afraid of him hurting me by staying. I'm afraid he'll destroy me if he leaves. We are a time bomb. I'm counting down the days till detonation, when I am left looking for my own foot in the wreckage.

"Why do you think I would hurt you?" he asks. I can't answer him without being brutally honest. *I don't know, because you have before?* Not answering me, but simply texting "no" because after all, we're not dating so I don't deserve politeness. I am just a slut, so I don't deserve an explanation. "I would never hurt you."

He brushes my hair out of my eyes. It's too dark in here for eye contact, but I can feel the trail of electricity his fingers leave on their way across my forehead.

"I believe you," I tell him, even though I don't believe in anyone anymore, not even myself.

"Can we go in the bathroom?" he asks, suddenly remembering that Owen is asleep on the couch beside us.

"I don't care," I say.

"Now, baby, don't be like that," he says. *Like what?* It has been my answer since the beginning. What's your favorite position? *I don't care.* What time is too late to call you? *I don't care.* What do you wanna watch? *I don't care.* I let you run the show because then maybe you'd let me be your leading lady. But after a while sacrifice starts to look a lot like apathy. Martyrs have no place in his world. We stumble off towards the bathroom. I hardly stub my toe in the dark. This apartment was my second home for most of sophomore year, I can navigate it with my eyes closed, I know each floorboard by heart.

There's a long hallway to the bathroom, lined with shelves of paper towels, 409, Lysol, the supplies for if the cops come, clean up and hide. This hallway has always reminded me of Alice's rabbit hole, the drunker you are, the longer it gets. Tonight though, the hall is all too short. I walk into the bathroom and flip on the light. I pull myself up onto the bathroom sink and stare up at Rich. He is sparrow thin with marijuana leaf boxers. Sometimes when I look at him, I can see him twenty years from now: a receding hairline, knobby wrists and a PBR can in his fist. He will be the type of father that would cuss out his child's teacher during parent conferences. I shake my head. I will not know Rich then. But for now I'm sitting on the bathroom sink with him in between my thighs. We're looking each other in the eye, wondering what we're still doing here.

"Turn around," he says. He pulls me off the counter, frantic like the thing's on fire, like I might disappear up in smoke before his eyes. "I wanna hit it from the back." What is this "it" he is always talking about? Is "it" me? Or something separate, an extension of myself but with its own soul, like a barnacle clinging onto a rock? Whatever "it" is— he seems to love 'it' more than he will ever love me. I'm just a third wheel, getting dragged along for the ride.

I'm holding myself up off the ground by rooting my hands through the countertop. I know this floor too well. I have slept on it in helpless and happier days. But I am above it now, with Rich smashing my head into the mirror, accidentally.

"Am I hurting you?" he pauses, it's calm, but it's as uneasy as sitting in the eye of a tornado. The girl glaring at me from the mirror is puffy faced and red eyed. Her breath comes in uneven splashes of rum flavored fog against the glass. I know now who "it" is. I'm staring her in the eye, this girl with her underwear looped around her ankles and her shoulders shaking from having to hold her own.

"No," I say because I want the worst for her, this monster staring back at me. I want her to go up in pieces with mirror chunks and seven years of shitty luck, because maybe then I'll be able to start again.

But he's through too soon and my demon's breath still clouds up my face in the looking glass. He brings me back down to earth and tells me to pull up my underwear up before we hit the living room, as if I had any decency left to hide from his friends.

Take me home, I wanna tell him as we tumble back onto the pull out couch, because it's three am and I can name every ghost that walks these walls. Take me home because you're leaving again tomorrow on another work trip, and I'll be gone to camp in a week. Take me home because I'm tripping over Mountain Dew cans and we're sleeping on a pull out couch and this is as close to the trailer park as I ever want to get. He's got his arm thrown over me, his head resting in the hollow of my neck. We feign in sleep a tenderness we never share in life. I am cuddled into a lie. I haven't heart left enough for dead ends, and I already know this is going nowhere.

He's celebrating his last night of freedom, but I couldn't care less. After tonight, I will never see Rich again. I will not be around to see his sentencing, will never know the difference if it was community service or incarceration. I don't give a damn either way, by his side I'm already in jail. "I'm innocent," I mouth to the midnight room, but I'm not sure I can even convince myself of that anymore.

***

The man's name was Charlie MacArthur, a reporter and a bad boy. Dorothy found herself head over heels for him. She was just a drop in the bucket, one of his many. Things did not go according to plan. Dorothy would never have any trouble getting a man; keeping him, however, was something else entirely. The pair separated just in time for Dorothy to find herself pregnant with Charlie's child. She had a choice: raise a fatherless child in the unforgiving decade of the 1920's, with no family, no husband to help her, or she could opt out. Abortion wasn't legal, but it wasn't impossible either. Dorothy decided she couldn't do this alone.

Dorothy was a gifted poet but no mathematician. She hadn't counted the weeks quite right and the fetus she aborted looked more like a fully formed infant than the clump of cells she had been told it would be. Dorothy watched in absolute horror as the last testimony of her love for Charlie was hacked into pieces and torn from her. She couldn't seem to get the scene out of her head. She'd close her eyes and see a wisp of hair, a sleepily curled and dimpled fist. She had always wanted a child, just not this child, not this time.

Her witty retorts at the round table were replaced by bloody recounts of her unborn child's murder to all that would listen. People began to grow sick of her morbidity. They looked at her with pity rather than laughter as she continued to throw out the same punchline over and over. *That's what I get for putting all my eggs in one bastard.* It wasn't funny anymore. People don't really know what to do with tragedy, not really. It's great for art, but not much for conversation. It gives you just enough rope, sometimes.

Dorothy began to drink, scotch for breakfast. She buckled under the weight of her lobotomy heavy grin. People would wince at how it never seemed to match her tear stung eyes. Dorothy felt herself to be dying, but she couldn't stop smiling, had to keep laughing with the desperation of a lunatic giggling into the echoing halls of a madhouse. This is what the people that knew her expected of her.

One night, after ordering take out, Dorothy Parker decided that she'd rather not stay alive

to answer the door for the delivery boy. Smiling, even for one more person, seemed too Herculean an effort for her to bare. She shut herself up in the bathroom. Her cartoon eyes floated down to the counter, to the shaving razor that Eddie had left behind, an artifact of a past life that she could not seem to bring herself to throw away. Now she saw it as a tool. A key. She would escape. Be free of all of this. Finally. She would later blame the entire incident on poor bumbling Eddie. If he had just not left his things lying about, then maybe none of this would have happened at all. Really, he was just so careless.

The delivery boy discovered Dorothy lying in a pool of her own blood as red as her baby doll lips. The slashes at her wrists could have almost been mistaken for ribbons. It would have been a more logical explanation, rather than such a pretty thing committing such an ugly act.

But she lived, despite her best advice or judgment. She wore her bandages like Tiffany bracelets back out into society. Her friends at the round table didn't know how to talk around the subject. They had never known anyone else who had attempted such a thing before. Dorothy became a reluctant resident expert. Dorothy cursed herself for not even being able to do this final thing right. She wrote out her resume in a poem. Shrugged. She figured she might as well live. She couldn't seem to succeed, even at giving up. This was just her luck.

**

I tumbled down the stairs into the gray mouth of a Christmas morning one year. My child feet, secure in the toes of their footsie pajamas muffled their way through the living room, to the kitchen. The feet of the Christmas tree were awash with presents. This was a side effect my father had from growing up with nothing. He felt as though he had to give us everything, even if we didn't want it. I checked the kitchen counter, saw that Santa Claus had eaten all the pickled eggs and drank all the beer that we had left out for him the night before. I reassured myself that I had gone yet another year without being forgotten.

I swung open the coffee mug cupboard, retrieved our tiny statue of baby Jesus from his hiding place. I cradled the tiny porcelain baby in the palm of my hand, kissed him on his impossibly small forehead.

"Happy Birthday," I whispered before placing him on the floor of our family's manger scene, where his porcelain mother and stepfather had been patiently waiting for his arrival, standing silent vigil for the entire month of December.

Phillip chirped from across the kitchen, from atop the jelly cabinet where my mother had banished the birdcage. I fumbled sleepily over to the cage, a Merry Christmas swishing between my baby teeth for the both of them, my happy couple in their home within my home.

This morning the bird cage was a crime scene. Annica's feathers dusted the floor of it, as silent and thick as Christmas snow. Her body, still and plucked pink and bare lay sprawled, her wings spread as crucifix wide. I was young, but I was old enough to recognize death when I saw it. I looked back at Phillip, where he swung, happily singing to himself on his perch. He paused, cocked his head. He eyed me coldly, as if to take responsibility, but not to beg forgiveness. Something inside my young and hopeful bones snapped. I wanted justice, retribution, a reason and accounting for all blood shed. I was not old enough yet to realize that the universe did not owe me these things, that so much in life lives and dies without explanation.

My dimpled fists hooked on to the bars of that old Victorian cage and shook, a small god tantruming an earthquake into being. I shook the cage until Phillip squawked back in protest, until birdseed spilled across the floor of the cage, burying Annica, showering her like rice being thrown across the shoulders of a bride. I shook the cage until Phillip, like Annica once had, wished only for escape. He clawed desperately at the doors that bound him, but the pipecleaners held fast.

"Bad, bad birdie," I shrieked until I could hear my mother's feet hitting the floor in the other room. "Bad, bad birdie."

My mother, with my brother taut as a bowling ball beneath her skin, ran to me, grabbed

My arms and hugged them to my side. The baby that would be my brother wedged his way into my side as she hugged me, reminding me of all the distance between people, even as they held me close.

"He killed her Mama," I cried, my face hot and tear spattered. "He killed her."

My mother stroked my hair, made shushing noises between her teeth. "He loved her to death," Mama justified. "That's all."

I peeked back at the cage, a haunted house looking thing looming down at me from atop the jelly cabinet. No, Mama must have had it wrong. Love was not supposed to be this ugly. Love was not meant to be violent. Love was not meant to look anything like a gamble.

Phillip had come to land at the bottom of the cage. He nudged Annica's body with his stop light beak as if he expected her to resurrect for him, to rise up and sing sweet songs with him as they once had.

We shuffled Annica's hollow and crumpled bones into a candy tin, buried her beneath the tree in the backyard that held my swing. Despite the cold, I sat my pajama bottoms on the wooden board of it, clasped my frost pricked fingers around the ropes that dangled down from the branches like hangman's nooses in the gray morning. I kicked my feet, pumping until my lungs sat barbed wire stern in my chest, until I tasted penny copper blood on my breath. I closed my eyes and wondered what it was to fly without having to worry about being thrown back to the Earth. I wondered if Annica had ever felt that free. I wondered if I ever would either.

My father was trying to buy me a lifetime. Instead, he bought me a cage, taught me that they come in all shapes and sizes and sometimes they even look like houses. My father had wanted me to know love as a pretty thing with feathers. Unfortunately, that never worked out quite right.

How to Die

When Adam, the boy you have loved since Freshman year, tells you that he will never love you, contrary to what you have so long believed, you will not die.

You will, however, have to remind yourself not to cry at the bar, in front of strangers. You will loop your fingers around Shane's boyfriend's brother's ears and kiss him full on the mouth in front of Adam. You will drink to forget Adam, the first man, the first sinner, the destroyer of God-given paradises. You will drink not one, but three long island iced teas, forcing the bartender to cut you off due to a not so fond memory of you puking on the bar room couch over the summer. You will overcome this minor setback by finishing other people's drinks that they have left unattended around the pool table or by allowing the boy you have just kissed to buy drinks for you.

The boy's name is Avery. He will watch your bubble gum mouth intently for the next two hours as you drunkenly explain to him exactly everything that was wrong with the depiction of Harley Quinn in the recent *Suicide Squad* movie. You will try to remind yourself that not even Harley lived happily ever after with her joker. But, she moved on, bought a roller rink and started dating Poison Ivy. You will briefly consider becoming a lesbian.

You will smoke more cigarettes tonight than you have ever smoked collectively in your entire life. You want to burn the house of your body to the ground. The boy will sit across from you at the outdoor picnic table, holding your free hand. He will look like he is falling in love in the August night. You are falling apart, totally and completely. You keep checking the air above your head for a mushroom cloud, but you can't tell because of all the cigarette smoke.

The boy eventually asks you if you want to get out of here. He means, of course, get out of this bar. You say yes, because you do want to get out of "here", out of this town, out of this state, out of this body and out of your mind.

You walk home, with the boy's hand in yours. You look at the stars, your reflection in the roadside puddles, anything but the boy. If you do not look at him, you can still pretend that this hand attached to yours is Adam's. Nevermind that Adam always had a history of holding everything but your hand. A car bumping trap music skims by. A white man in a flat brim yells out the window some unoriginal comment about your ass. You toss your hair and stick your tongue out before flipping the fading headlights the finger.

"That happen to you a lot?" The boy asks. You nod, like this privilege of beauty is something you carry heavy as a cross about your shoulders. The boy smiles, like he's winning at something, like he's any better than that man in the car because he's holding your hand. You want to tell him that you are not a prize, you are a fucking plague, a God sent punishment and rapture. But you are feeling more black widow than lunar moth tonight, so you kiss him on the sidewalk and give him another reason to smile.

When you get back to the apartment, he can't get it up, too much alcohol, nerves, maybe. You will not tell anyone about this the next day when Shane asks you what happened. Because of this small kindness, he will revere you as something bordering on sainthood. You will love being thought of as something holy to somebody and allow him to stay. In the months coming, it will be important to look back and remember, that even in the beginning, this relationship was built on the pimpled back of a white lie.

You spend the night sitting on the floor of your bedroom, making him listen to unreleased Lana Del Rey songs about trailer parks and motel rooms and dangerous girls. You tell him stories about your life up until this point, a grocery list of heart wrenching hookups, bottles bled dry and tattoos in promiscuous places. He doesn't flinch, like other people do when you speak. You like this about him, if nothing else.

He matches you story for story. The truth pops apart like stitches when he opens his mouth, like it's something that has been itching at him for a while, a wound he can't seem to hide or heal.

He had seen a girl go up in flames once from where she sat in the driver's seat of a pick up truck. She had been too drunk to drive, too drunk to run from the wreckage. It all happened too fast. There had been nothing to do but watch her skin melt into the steering wheel. When he tells you this, you have a sudden urge to put out the flames behind his eyes. You can see fire in the jaws of his pupils, consuming everything. You think that maybe, he will be the death of you someday, someway. And you smile at this possibility.

As the alcohol dims, you can see him for what he is, a skinny white boy with night black hair and a Mountain Dew grin. You think this looks like happiness the way that aspartame looks like sugar. It has a bit of an aftertaste, but it's nothing you don't think you could get used to.

A month later you will wake up with Avery beside you. You will stand in front of the mirror in your room and comb your fingers through your hair, desperately trying to keep it from dreadlocking. Your hair has always been just as stubborn as you are.

"You're beautiful," Avery will say because he means it. Because he has a habit of looking at you like you are the second coming, with awe and always a little bit of fear. He dots his sentences with needless apologies, as though your relationship were built on trip wires, as if one wrong step could blow the whole thing up in his face.

"Really? Even with my troll hair?" you will ask in disbelief.

"All the time, babe," he will say, hugging you from the back. You look in the mirror at what should look like bliss. Instead the sight sends hairline fractures cascading through your soul. You are always afraid when you are happy. It means that you have something to lose.

Being with Avery is waiting for a cavity to form. He is too sweet for you, you know he is rotting your armor, but he tastes good just the same. He is corroding your resolve, eating away at your composure from the inside out, so that when he leaves you, as they all do eventually, you won't have any teeth to bite back with. He is slowly turning you into the girlfriend type.

You begin to think maybe it's enough in this world to love someone and have somebody love you. Whoever said that they had to be the same person?

The Girlfriend's Guide to Anger Management

Samson loved Delilah. Delilah loved her reflection in Samson's eyes. Samson was the strongest man in their village, he could win any fight, run any distance. Delilah even once witnessed him lifting a camel because it was blocking his path in the road. Samson was so strong that sometimes it frightened Delilah.

Delilah was an imperfect, beautiful woman with hair the color of sunlit desert sand and eyes as blue and restless as the ocean. Delilah had nomad eyes, always wandering to places where they didn't belong. Delilah loved only her reflection and attention, wherever she could find it. It proved to her that she existed at all, a question she would often pose to herself as she stared down the bare and tiny horizon past their ever smaller village.

Delilah felt trapped between the leering line of that ever tightening horizon and Samson's too strong arms. Delilah would watch the sun dip down past the dirt and sigh. She'd stumble back into their tent and lay with Samson's too-strong arm draped across her chest. She fell asleep wondering when Samson would notice her too-wandering eyes. His arm stared up at her in the dark like a lion peeking through the bushes, peaceful now, but what would it do if it were angry? In the dark she watched her breath rise and fall against the confines of Samson's body. How much longer? She couldn't breathe.

***

It is witching weather. The clouds hang low to the ground weighed down by heavenly burden, so low that I worry about scraping my head against them, in spite of myself. I hunch my shoulders, bow my head against the empty threat of rain. A warm breeze blows dead leaves around us. It's like a snow globe, but everything is dying. Except for me and Avery, who sits beside me on the park bench, staring at the traffic.

We became official last Wednesday, and I'm still trying to get used to the idea. I wear his love like a gifted dress, pretty, I'm sure, for somebody, but I'm not sure it's what I would have picked out. He has riot teeth, all pushing and shoving each other to be up front. The specters of sideburns cut down the sides of his too-small head like blades. A nonsense tribal tattoo spills its way down one of his forearms. He is too skinny. I'd waited for love for most of my life; I had not expected this to be what it looked like.

He doesn't eat breakfast. I do. There's hummus from my bagel caking up under my fingernails. I have always been anxious about eating in front of people so I take bites bigger than my mouth is wide, trying to get this over with quickly. I am biting off more than I can chew in more ways than one.

"I think Emmett and Shane broke up because she was always going out on girls night," Avery says. We are discussing his brother's break up with my best friend. She was my reason for dating him to begin with. And now, he is dissecting her every decision like a high school biology frog. This is the way our outings go, he talks and I nod along and sometimes, if I'm lucky, I squeeze a word in edgewise, something small and bite size like "yeah" or "definitely". Nothing too hard to swallow.

"Why would anyone want a girls' night? Why would you wanna go out and be gawked at by anyone who's not their boyfriend?" he asks, rhetorically.

A quarter sized drop of hummus slips past the tinfoil in my fist and splats on the park bench between us, just barely missing my fishnet covered legs. My phone sits in my purse like a tell tale heart with a message from an old flame. Adam messaged me last night, breaking two months of silence like a promise. He'd told me in August I was not what he wanted. Now it seemed he was changing his mind. Now that it was too late.

"I don't know," I tell Avery, dabbing the bench, as if anyone cared.

"That's one thing that there's absolutely no excuse for, no turning back from," Avery's face turns to stone, I can see his knuckles blooming white, trying to poke through the skin of his clenched fists. "Cheating."

"I would never do that to you," I say, making enough eye contact to see the storm of a memory behind his pupils. I crumple up my remaining half of bagel like a failed test. I'm no longer hungry. I'm left feeling accused of something I haven't even done yet.

***

My mother's grandfather escaped Nazi-invaded Poland. He wrapped his too long Jewish name in butcher paper at the American border and drowned whatever part of it he no longer needed in the Atlantic Ocean. Great Grandfather never talked about Poland, never talked about the family he left behind. When I asked about them, as a child, he would shrug and tell me in heavily accented English that he had been raised by wolves. It wasn't a hard thing to believe. He was a jealous man, hungry man, mean man. He was not a smart enough man to believe that other people could be anything but what he was.

His wife, Bertha, was a Jewish princess, an hourglass body, eyes goldfish big and black as the grave. Her coffee ground hair tumbled and curled down her back, long and rambling as a back road. Great Grandfather and Bertha lived in a shanty, tin roof, dirt poor, five dogs, all teeth and chain link fence vicious barking from what little yard they had. Bertha was the only thing of value that Great Grandfather owned. She was the only golden thing salvaged from the war. He lived in constant fear that she would leave him, that he would be left with nothing but the snarl of German Shepherds, just as he had been back home.

Bertha couldn't speak English. Bertha had only attended enough school to learn to write. She had nowhere to run to even if she had wanted to. Great Grandfather never understood that she didn't want to.

***

A certain serpent smelled Delilah's desperation on the wind, a smell like frying bacon and fresh brewed coffee. Delilah's desperation smelled like opportunity, so the serpent came a slithering to her garden. And what did the serpent want with Delilah? Well, Samson was not only the strongest man in all the village, but also their most powerful and bravest warrior. He was fearless because he was invincible and on any given day, he was often the only thing standing between God's chosen people and a quick demise at the hands of their enemies. Now you see why Satan had any interest at all in Delilah? Evil has very little interest in beauty for beauty's sake. They're more interested in what they can do with it.

Regardless, while Delilah mournfully watered the kale plants every morning as the sun wrapped it's lazy fingers about her shoulders, the serpent would croon; "Hey there Delilah…"

"What?" she'd snap. Snakes were *not* her type.

"Samson's so strong," Satan hissed.

"Yeah, I know," she'd reply, bored. People noticed Samson's strength more often than her beauty, and it had begun to gnaw at her nerves.

"He's stronger than me. He's sure as hell stronger than you. Maybe even stronger than God," the serpent listed.

"Well he sure seems to think so," Delilah pouted.

"You are far from perfect, Delilah," the serpent hissed, his ribbon tongue tracing the outline of her ear. "You make many mistakes, and often."

"I'll chop your mouth off with the garden hoe!" Delilah threatened, although she didn't move. She was the center of attention, and so she sat still, hypnotized.

"What if Samson were to find out? Got mad at you?" the serpent taunted. "Why my dear, he could snap you in half like a toothpick. You've got many a pretty feature, love, but at the end of the day, you're no match for him."

Panic clawed at the back of Delilah's throat. In that moment, she could see the outline of every man's hand who wasn't Samson printed against her honey skin. Traced in blood. She pulled her shawl about her in shame, sure that anyone who passed could surely see this mark of Cain about her, too.

"Please serpent," she begged. "What must I do?"

The serpent smiled a smile unnaturally wide and toothy for a snake. The vines of the string bean plants unfurled their coiled fingers and dropped a pair of iron scissors into Delilah's outstretched and desperate hands.

"Just a little haircut should do the trick," the serpent said.

***

"Avery, slow down!" I gasp, as we take another sharp corner Tokyo Drift style. Avery's fists are white knuckled around the wheel like it's the neck of something he's trying to strangle. His jaw is clenched so tightly that I'm listening in the tense silence between us to hear his riot teeth snapping like guitar strings. I'm mouthing the words to a Hail Mary under my alcohol tinged breath.

"Don't tell me what to do!" he snaps. I wind the chain of my purse around my shaking fingers, lynch rope anxious. Tonight was supposed to be peaceful enough. Dinner with his family. A Chinese restaurant, his grandmother's birthday. A movie, sweet sex when we got back to his place, eventually. But now my expectations of a hopeful evening are splattered like the road kill squirrel we just passed. I can feel maggots already wriggling through the meat of it, eating away at any safety I felt beside him.

Three Blue Hawaiians in, Avery had mentioned Shane. Emmett's face had taken on the expression of a lame dog facing a gun. His grandmother had told Avery to shut his trap, to not be putting his nose in other people's wounds. Avery flipped a table.

"You need to figure your shit out," I scream. "Otherwise I can't do this." I think of my Mamere's too small frame beside my Papere's too loud anger. About how she was always drinking plain hot water, a diet tip, to be smaller. She couldn't afford to take up anymore room; the house was already full to bursting with his temper. I would not make my voice small for Avery. I have a temper too.

I look over and see that there are tears coming out of his bloodshot eyes. I contemplate jumping out the car door. In the middle of main street. In the rain. I did not sign on to be his therapist. I am not getting paid to be his babysitter on these tantrum sprees. I want out.

"I'm sorry," he says, repeating it like the sheer multitude of the words will bring him penance. I want to tell him that nothing he has ever said to me in any way resembled a Hail Mary. He shouldn't try to start now.

We pull into my driveway. The blackened windows of my empty apartment glare down at me like hungry eyes, threatening to swallow me whole. Suddenly the tantrum, the crying, my fear pooling up in sweat under my armpits means nothing. I can't spend the night alone. It's pathological, it's irrational and it's impending. I can feel the hot breath of lonely on my neck. I panic. I reach across the center council to kiss Avery. I can taste his tears in my mouth. Gutted McDonald's bags crunch beneath my feet. I pull away and his face loosens for a moment, a marionette cut free from its strings. For a moment, there is hope.

"Come on up?" I plead. "It'll be fun. I promise?"

Anger drops back over his face swift as the blade of a guillotine.

"I bet it would," he says. "But I think it's best that I go home."

I pop open the car door and step out into the rain slashed October night. The point of my heel sinks into the heart of a puddle. I watch Avery's tail lights disappear past the trailer park, then the liquor store and finally around the bend of the fairgrounds. There are no more cars on the road. If I were to scream, would anyone hear me? Would anybody care? I flip my own table. I text Adam.

***

Great Grandfather was too pessimistic to see Bertha's happiness. He always felt that her smile was built on melting ice and not pearls. He always felt her laughter was a promise that she had made to somebody else. He never quite believed that something so beautiful could belong to him. Great Grandfather didn't believe in good things coming; he didn't believe in God. The only thing truly Jewish about him was his nose. The only gospel he knew was that of the clenched fist, the sharp tongue, the chain link fence. Bertha was too kind hearted to see any of these things in him.

Bertha was inexplicably lonely. Only one other person in their bumpkin New York town spoke Polish. Unfortunately for him, he was a man, the owner of the general store downtown. Bertha loved to talk. She was always more in love with the sound of her voice than she had ever been in love with Great Grandfather. Bertha began loitering at the general store. Bertha would lean her back road curls and her hourglass chest over the counter to talk to the Polish-tongued man. She would spin stories that sounded like home to her. She would laugh like God. It was innocent, kid stuff. The only time she ever touched the Polish-tongued man was when he was handing her change back to her, his calloused hands brushing the worn silk of her kid gloves.

That was not what Great Grandfather saw. Great Grandfather was a quick trigger man. He had a merry-go-round of beds he visited, the pull out couches of shanty girls, the canopy curtained mattresses of townhouse ladies, the bathroom stalls of bar floozies. He was the talk of the town, a talk all in English that went right over Bertha's head. She would never understand what he truly was. And Great Grandfather was never smart enough to imagine that anyone could ever be anything better from what he was, not even his darling Bertha.

***

Little did Delilah know that Samson's hair had never been cut. God had instructed him never to under any circumstances cut his hair or his strength would be gone before he could even brush the split ends off his shoulders.

What Delilah knew, but was too insecure to believe, was that Samson absolutely and truly wouldn't lay a pinky on her. He knew every transgression. He could trace every line she ever crossed with his big toe. He didn't care how many ways she broke his heart, being with her, vain, selfish, beautiful her on her worst days was still better than his best days without her.

He'd pray to God all the time. *Please forgive Delilah for her evils, she knows not what she does.* God would shake his head at Samson and say, "Boy, you gotta quit her. That girl is gonna be the death of you."

But Samson, although strong like a bull, was as dumb as an ox. He always took what God said as a figure of speech. Until the day when of course, it proved not to be anymore.

***

"Come over," Adam texts, out of the midnight hopeless. This is new. Usually he comes to me. I haven't seen where Adam lives since the beginning of it all, way back during Freshman year, and I am terrified I will be disappointed with it now. God has a guest list for heaven for a reason. What if it doesn't live up to the hype anymore?

Avery is still puking "I'm sorries" up all over my phone like a college Freshman at a kegger. I tell him I already have my dad, I do not need another angry man in my life. I don't tell him that *angry* is the only type of man I'm into. I am not offended by his anger, it makes me homesick in all the right ways. I am offended because he cried.

I leave the phone on my bed, a comforter that still smells like Avery: Twisted Tea, cheap weed and dollar store cologne. I won't need him where I'm going.

The kitchen is empty, silent as a ghost town. Two mason jars are lined up on the kitchen table, mint leaves dying in the bellies of each one. The veins of these petals are swollen and dried from a mojito they had soaked up the Saturday before. My roommate, Bianca, had handed me one of the jars the way she did with most things, as if she were trying to teach me how to live. "This is what we would drink in Cuba," she had said, a Vera Bradley headband bobbing in her unwashed hair in time with her words. I had sipped, I had chugged trying to get a taste for a land I would never know. It had gone down like water- not nearly strong enough. Last Saturday I had needed an exorcism, not a baptism. Last Saturday I was trying to drown Adam and his untimely texts, still trying to resurrect myself in Avery's image. I had needed fire in my throat, a storm in my brain so that I could no longer say Adam's name, let alone remember what it was. And maybe it's this need for burning, for hurricane, that draws me back to him now. Bianca is not home tonight to try to tell me how to live, has no weak advice or drinks to give me now. There's no one home to hear the front door open. No one there to tell me not to go. No friend to talk me down. They expect this from me by now, and I wonder sometimes if I act out for the benefit of my own self interest, or if I am just trying to live up to their stereotype of me.

There is antifreeze Blue Hawaiian clawing its way up the back of my throat. I consciously remind myself not to puke all over the rain sparked sidewalk. I don't have gum. I can't afford to show up with my breath tasting of vomit. There's no stars, no moon to guide me. I think of all the warnings my mother ever gave me about walking alone at night by myself. It is rural Maine, and I am already dating the worst thing you could run into in a dark alley around here. Where I am going is better than where I'm coming from. At least this is what I tell myself.

There is a gaggle of longboarders making their way down the road like some strange herd of animal. They glance sideways at me, but do not speak and I am grateful for their quiet. Through the trees, I can hear the groan of excavators and backhoes, sounding like dragons in the night. The bridge out of Farmington needs fixing. There are construction workers trying to build better ways out of here. And I hope with all my heart that they succeed.

My heels beat a staccato into the pavement. I hum along to a song about Ouija board lovers, men who only resurrect from the dead when their own lonely needs it's fill. Men like Adam, that would always feel like ghosts to me, even with their hands wrapped around my neck, insubstantial and fleeting. But I always saw more hope at funerals than at weddings. I sing along drunkenly to myself in the dark: *"The word distraught cannot describe how my heart has been. But where do we begin now that you're back from the dead."*

***

Great Grandfather loaded his Winchester on a Saturday morning, when more devout Jews would be praying to more worthy gods in synagogues elsewhere. But their bumpkin town didn't have a temple. Great Grandfather didn't try to conceal his shotgun, just walked down main street with the barrel gleaming against his weather beaten Levis, his mouth set into a line as serious and thin as the border he had crossed to get to this country in the first place.

The bell posted above the door tinged, announcing Great Grandfather's arrival at the general store. The Polish-tongued man had time to plea for mercy in the same language he had used to supposedly woo Great Grandfather's wife, before the first shot rang out. A woman screamed from behind stacks of flour, a mother hid her baby in the side of her coat hoping that wool could stop bullets. The gun rang out five more times as Great Grandfather emptied the entire clip into the Polish-tongued man's left foot. The man would never walk again, but he would live. Great Grandfather cocked his gun, the empty shells twinkling like wedding bells as they hit the floor. He calmly walked out onto the front porch of the general store. He took a seat on the porch swing, slung the Winchester into his lap like the leg of a faithful lover and patiently waited for the police to come bring him home.

***

Delilah kept the scissors in her pillow case. She slept on them for a week, turning it over in her mind. She did love Samson, in her own twisted and emotionally constipated way. She didn't want to hurt him. But wouldn't she love a Samson that she could manage, *more*? Wouldn't she love a Samson free of consequence, *more*?

One night, she could not bear the weight of the blades beneath her skull any longer. She waited for Samson to fall to snoring against her collarbone. He fell asleep like this every night, with his arm clasped around her so that she couldn't even roll over if she wanted to. He called it love. She called it suffocating.

She twirled a yard of Samson's hair between her fingertips. She stared at the strand as if it were a cliff she were considering jumping from. She held her breath, then snapped the mouth of the scissors over the hair like the teeth of some hungry animal. She held the amputated lock in her fist. She snipped another and another and another. By the time Samson's eyes drifted open, Delilah had an entire bouquet of his hair clenched in her tiny fist.

Samson blinked for a moment, then lifted his hand to his now bare scalp. His own arm was almost too heavy a thing for him to lift. The reality of the situation was almost too much for him to believe.

"Delilah? What have you done?" Delilah dropped the scissors and the hair in the dirt, startled by the tone of voice on Samson's lips. He'd never raised his voice to her before, had never been angry with her before. "You've ruined us! What have you done!"

***

"My favorite was always Hyde," I admit. Adam and I are making small talk, and I have no GPS for this type of situation. We're watching *That 70's Show* because that's usually what I watch while I am waiting for him. In my own bed. At home. Now I am waiting for him to finish the joint he is smoking from his perch on the windowsill. His bed has an oddly childish sports themed comforter, bats and baseballs cascading off into the abyss of a blue backdrop. I cringe, I had not noticed this the first time I was here, three years ago.

I am kicking myself, *really Liza? The "love of your life" is a 22 year old man that still lives on campus?* Adam's room looks no different than the first time I saw it three years ago. Same Marilyn Monroe and Malcolm X posters staring me down from the cinder block walls. Same fan blowing everything illegal smelling out the window. I wonder how much of who I am, who I have become throughout my college career, actually has to do with my own preferences and how much has to do with the pursuit of him. Liking certain things so that maybe someday…

"Donna was always my favorite," he tells me after a large inhale. My heart sinks, if I had just been myself around him, three years ago, instead of trying to be what I thought he wanted, maybe he would've seen the brainy badass girl the inside of my head tells me I am. But it's too late now. And I don't care.

Adam answered the front door of his building in nothing but his boxers. He is collecting a beer gut that makes his six foot frame look too much like a question mark for me. His face looks older now without his ever present sunglasses. I wonder if I too, look this harsh in the light of day. Were we always destined to be mirrors? I shake loose the thought. If I am being optimistic, I can call him nothing but friend now. This is not about love, about a three year sense of misplaced longing anymore. This is revenge. This will be the last time I ever see Adam. It's funny how the things we once claimed that we would die for, burn cities for, sacrifice first born children for, fade into the backdrop so easily. Maybe we just get tired. Or maybe we just get smarter.

"So are you gonna tell me what happened?" he asks. We are a weird type of friendship but it's there, every once in awhile, when the smoke clears.

"My boyfriend got us kicked out of a Chinese place," I say, not really wanting to go deeper into it than that. "I'm not sure how much longer this is gonna last."

"Sounds like he doesn't have what it takes," he says. He kisses me then, with a mouth born of Marlboros and discount whiskey. Adam doesn't have what it takes either, and he knows it, doesn't want to, to begin with. He offers me nothing but hopelessness and lonely and his tobacco stained hand in my shirt.

Fucking him is like making love to a ghost. There was life here once, but that was long ago and now I'm left attempting to entertain a corpse. I don't know how to fit into his arms anymore. I forgot in his self imposed exile of two months that he doesn't like kissing me. What have I done playing with Ouija boards? Am I to be haunted now because I never had the heart to bury the dead? I think about fucking Avery, how it always seemed like I was looking for repentance or an exorcism.

I'm screwing Adam even though this isn't fun anymore. My heart no longer skips a beat when I see him. My soul recoils, shrivels like the dying petal of a November rose because this means that I no longer love anything. But we're still here. Isn't that the definition of addiction? When you keep dancing even though you're dizzy and you're afraid you're bound to fall? Isn't that the word for the people who keep dancing even though the music stopped years ago, even though you can no longer remember the words to the song? A word for all those people that could never seem to hear the universe screaming at them to stop. Adam and I had always had our headphones up too loud, our parents had always warned us that we would go deaf at an early age. We couldn't hear anyone tell us stop. We wouldn't listen to anyone tell us no.

Adam is as drunk as me, I realize, halfway through hooking up, when he slurs, "Do you think I could make it down South? Like anywhere but here?"

He is and has always been an out of place puzzle piece, a *Straight Outta Compton* enthusiast in backwoods Maine. He catches me off guard sometimes by asking me these big life questions at unexpected times. I never know what he wants from me. I never know how to answer.

"What?" I say, pretending I hadn't heard. I never could give him what he wanted. And maybe that's why we fell apart and continue to do so so fucking often. Because I don't know how to listen. Because maybe all this time, he thought I hadn't cared.

"Nothing," he says, the mask of his typical attitude dropping back down. "How does this feel?" he asks pushing a little deeper.

"Amazing," I breathe.

"Then I guess that's all that matters."

***

Great Grandfather got five years in Attica State Penitentiary. The prison that housed him would later birth a riot; men would die here. I like to think that it was Great Grandfather's anger that poisoned this place, that when he left they couldn't seem to scrub all of his meanness out of their cinder block walls. His rage had soaked through the concrete floor and planted something deep and evil there.

Bertha never completely understood what he had done or why they had to be apart. She stayed dumbly faithful to him all through his incarceration. She wrote him a letter every day. She didn't know that Great Grandfather had never learned to read. Bertha never knew how to recognize lost causes. She was the type of woman that would marry a death row inmate and still be optimistic that there could still be a chance for them. I suppose this is where I get it from, this clinging on to things so long after they are clearly marked for death.

Bertha still tried to make conversation with the Polish-tongued man when she went

to buy dog food or flour. He would only look down at his one remaining foot and act as though her language wasn't one he understood anymore. Great Grandfather had finally gotten exactly what he was looking for. Bertha now spoke to no one but him.

***

Delilah did not see Samson captured as easily as a child being lifted by a parent. Delilah did not see him chained to pillars in a strange city, by a strange people. She did not hear him ask God with his dying breath to forgive her, for she knew not what she had done. Delilah did not hear Samson say that he loved her for the last time. Delilah did not see the pillars crumble as Samson raged against his chains. She did not see him harness his last drop of strength to destroy the city of their enemies and himself with it. She did not see him die to keep her safe. Delilah did not see Samson's skull crushed and broken scattered among the bones of strangers.

Delilah was too busy mourning the fact that he had chosen to love her at all.

***

I blink myself awake into the next morning with Adam's grave dirt eyes staring back at me.

"Bien matin," I say in the language of my father, because all the English my tongue owns is still tied up in sleep.

"Buenos dias," he responds in Spanish, words he scavenged from minimum-wage kitchens and neighborhoods far from here, without missing a beat. We have always understood each other's lunacy, despite the fact that we dream in different languages. His lips brush mine, but in the sober light of day, I am remembering all the reasons this is wrong. I have become like him: a cheat. We were always destined to be mirrors. Separate but alike, uncanny. I don't kiss back.

I shake my head into the hollow of his collarbone. He shrugs, gives himself a hand job as I lay in his arms, motionless and dumb as a doll. And this is a blasphemy to everything we once were. This is the loneliest sight I have ever seen. Two people together, touching and naked, but worlds apart. I have never felt so alone. I am learning all the ways this will never look like love.

I fumble my way home from Adam's dorm room, awash in a dawn that is too bright, too hopeful for me. I think it is important to remember, that in the end, I was the one to walk away from him, even if it was only situational. I walk into my apartment, to the bathroom that has no lock. I sling my leg over the wall of the bathtub, turn the shower on. I stand there, fully clothed, staring up at the downpour as it bleeds through all my lace and denim. I wonder absently if anyone has ever drowned in the shower. I hold my breath, hold my head under the faucet and pray for either death or a baptism, whichever comes first. But I gasp, my mouth wretches itself open against my will. My body always has a bad habit of saving me from myself, even when I don't want it to.

I peel off my sopping clothes, splat them onto the floor outside the tub. I will forget them there, when I leave this afternoon. My roommate calls this careless, selfish. But those adjectives are getting obvious, redundant by now.

I'm using more body wash than I need, scrubbing until I can imagine I resemble the snake I truly am, limbless and sharp tongued, sloughing off this skin that I am so very tired of living in. I don't wash my hair though, it is tied up in a Rapunzel's ransom at the nape of my neck, safe from the water. Later, when I am fucking my boyfriend, the smell of Adam will still be woven around my skull like a halo I don't deserve.

There's a rash blooming like an angry rose in the garden of my left armpit. When the bible was fact, adulteresses were plagued with leprosy as punishment for their sins, a disease made noticeable by the presence of weeping and ghastly sores. The mark of Cain. I run my razor over the mottled skin and I am reminded of all that I have done.

It is 3 pm. Avery has lured me back into his fast food wrapper littered vehicle with the promise that he will, "make it up to me." There is a Twisted Tea can in his fist and a smile on his face as we pull out the drive, and so I believe him. My head is riding a wave of Blue Hawaiian hangover, and I am not in the mood to question any of it.

"Why do you always drink such sweet things if ya know it's gonna make you sick?" Avery asks me. I want to tell him that my life leaves enough of a bad taste in my mouth, that I don't need to add to it by sipping poison. But there is no simple way to explain this to the man who thought I slept alone last night, awaiting his apology like a sinner waits for absolution.

"I don't know, guess I'm an idiot," I say, because this is just how I feel today.

"No, I'm the idiot in this relationship," he says. I stay silent, because no one is about to contest this truth. Especially me, with someone else's mouth stamped in a hickey on the driver's side of my neck. The radio is off. I'm fishing through my purse to find my IPod to plug into the aux cable to cut the tension. The silence is dizzying. Avery has never dealt well with it.

"Wesley crashed his car last night," he says, referring to some friend of his I only met

once at the bar. The friend had been so high on cocaine that he ground his teeth like something possessed. For the first three weeks Avery talked about him, I was convinced the kid had cerebral palsy.

"Why? What happened?" I say in a voice of mock concern. I did four years of theater in high school. I can't even tell when I'm acting anymore.

"He and his girlfriend were fighting," he says, I can see the white sprouts of his knuckles

start to grow through the skin of his hand. His riot teeth clench ever so slightly. Maybe his smile wasn't as sure as I had betted on. The speedometer slowly creeps up to 55. "She grabbed the wheel while they were going 60."

"Well that wasn't smart," I say. "Why were they fighting?"

The speedometer is slowly creeping upward, 65, 70, 75. *Hail Mary full of grace…*

"She fucked some other guy at a party," Avery spits. *The lord is with thee.* He makes it sound like she deserved whatever came next. 80 mph. We go over a small hill, and I feel my stomach in my mouth. *Blessed art thou amongst women and blessed is the fruit of thy womb.*

Avery is no longer looking at the road, he's looking me dead in the eye. *Jesus.* Like he knows something. *Holy Mary, Mother of God.* I think briefly about grabbing the steering wheel, and diverting us from this course we're on. *Pray for us sinners.* But it's too late to turn back now.

Now and at the hour of our death. The car slows back to 70, then 60. Avery is not trying to kill us. He just wants to show me just how much of my life is in his hands.

Amen.

How to Fight

It is the weekend before Halloween, and you are at the sketchiest bar in town. The bar that has been shut down twice, just to open under a new name with the same exact problems: lack of ID checks, backroom cocaine, and a townie infestation. The bar has two half broken pool tables, a patchwork quilt square of a dance floor and a coin operated video game that allows you to shoot deer. A boy in a camo sweatshirt holds the plastic gun from the video game up to his friend's skull and jokingly pulls the trigger. Death is too common for it to be anything but a joke around people like Avery. The carpeted floor is studded with cigarette butts and used gum. You are terrified to see what has stuck to the soles of your heels.

Everyone assumes you are wearing a costume because everyone else is. The barroom is dotted with feather boas, fishnets and sugar skulls. You don't feel out of place. Tonight is the only night of the year that all the other girls dress exactly like you. Your boyfriend, who wears an under armor sweatshirt, too much Axe spray and a floppy grin, but no costume, introduces you to people he went to high school with. They try to guess what you are supposed to be in your black slip dress and fishnets. *Stripper? Marilyn Monroe? Flapper?* You shrug and say sure. At one point in time you have been all these things to all sorts of people. It had never felt like you were playing pretend before. But it feels like you're always wearing a costume lately. You have never been anybody's girlfriend before. It feels like somebody is going to pop out from behind every corner and yell, "gotcha!" before pulling the rug out from under your heels. And some small part of you, the part of you that ran to Adam last weekend, prays that they would.

You are bored or frightened around Avery unless you are startlingly drunk. You are now on your fifth vodka lemonade of the evening. You are singing "Closer" by the Chainsmokers louder than the jukebox. *Tell your friends it was nice to meet them, but I hope I never see them again.* Your boyfriend smiles at this, his Mountain Dew teeth peeking from between cracked lips. He assumes that you are imagining that the boy in the song is him. You don't know how to tell him that he will never be the boy in any of your love songs, so you take another drink. You pipe down. You shake the hand of another snaggletoothed white boy that will surely die in the same town he was born into, beside everyone else he went to high school with.

A girl with a septum piercing and an eat-your-heart-out look is kissing a bird nosed boy at the bar. The bird nosed boy is someone you have met briefly, one of Avery's buddies. His name is Ben, and he has an arrest record longer than your arm.

A blonde girl dressed like Luigi runs up behind Ben and Septum girl and punches their lips apart. You will learn later that the blonde is Ben's recent ex, when you get the full story, this sudden act of violence will make more sense. But for now, at the moment of impact, you imagine that you can hear teeth cracking like ice. But you think maybe it's just the facade shattering, the illusion that anyone has it together at all.

Septum girl knocks into the person seated at the barstool next to her on her way to the gum spackled floor. That person is dislodged from his barstool, and grabs the ass of some other man's girlfriend to keep himself from falling, or so he claims. The girlfriend and the man she belongs to punch the barstool man in sync as if they had counted it out together. A mosh pit of fists erupts against the shore of the bar.

"Stay here," your boyfriend tells you, before rushing into the fray, as if you would ever dream of another option. He is trying to save something, somebody else would think. But you know better by now, your boyfriend is only truly happy with someone else's blood under his fingernails. You watch the tiny blonde coil Septum's hair around her fist like spaghetti on a fork. Septum spits in her face and makes a move to bite her forearm.

You sip your lemonade. You click your ice around your glass absentmindedly. You hum along to a forgotten country song that spills out of the jukebox, *I've got friends in low places.* You marvel at all the crazy things that people do for love. You thank whatever god you still believe in that this is not something you care about anymore.

FEMA's Guide to Hurricane Season

Katrina's leaning against the front door of my boyfriend's house, smoking a cigarette, when I pull up the drive. I expected her to be there. Her guy friend lives here too. But every time I see her it's as if she popped out of a fairy tale. I'm scared to blink for fear she'll disappear. She's trashed already, at 7pm. You can see it in the way she's not really taking drags anymore, just kinda sitting there letting the cherry of her cigarette eat up her Walmart manicure. She's an amazon in heels. She's a queen, the half broken stoop of the front porch her throne. She stares stoically at the graveyard across the street, as if the headstones were her people. Her lips stand pursed as if she were about to make a decree.

A septum piercing peeks out defiantly between her nostrils. It makes me think of the bulls my father raises, the rings threaded through their sinuses so that you can lead them around on the threat of mutilation. These animals have horns that could run through a grown man, but with your finger looped through the ring, they're puppies on a leash. Katrina would not be led by anybody; she'd stab you first. Her hair is piled into a hairspray-riddled ponytail, trying desperately to cover the bald spot from her last bar fight. Her bottom lip is still fat from some other girl's fist.

"Baby girl!" she shrieks at me when I pop open the car door. "You're here! Now we can go to the bar!"

She's hugging me and pulling me out of the vehicle at the same time. I am her baby, child-sized in the shadow of her height. I push my bangs from my eyes. My babydoll slip is riding up, caught underneath her arm. It is November, snow is a rumor and it is too cold outside for what I am wearing. I'm struggling to lug my belongings to my boyfriend's house in a potato sack like a runaway child. Katrina tells me she loves me more often than my boyfriend does. I want to believe this as she shoves me through the front door. The door is half broken in and half-assedly patched up with a board. The board has a Sharpied smiley face across it, so it looks like the one from *Ed, Edd and Eddie*. My boyfriend had tried to make it a joke after he had kicked it in last week. We are always trying to patch up Avery's anger with laughter.

My boyfriend and his bros (biological and platonic) live in a house that could have maybe once been built with the intention of a nice family living in it. There are three bedrooms, a 1960s kitchen and a bathroom that looks like the one from *Pulp Fiction*. But everything seems to have strayed from its intentions. There are enough recyclables littered about to fund a class trip to NYC. The carpets, all white, are stained with God only knows what. I keep my socks on at all times. Avery says that he's heard people talking when no one is home but him, that door knobs wriggle when they shouldn't. The railing is split from the wall, and the stairs up to the second floor are too steep to climb them without trouble. This is my weekend home.

Avery stumbles down the stairs to meet me in the entryway. He presses a half frozen Twisted Tea can against my fishnet-covered thigh until I shriek and shove him. He loves to hear me scream.

"Hey babe," he speaks directly into my lips before he kisses me so that the inside of my throat echoes with his words. Avery is goofy with sideburns he is threatening to grow out. He is the kid from the MAD comic book all grown up. But he has the most intense blue eyes I have ever seen. A blue that could put drinks on the rocks. It's the blue of an empty mirror. If I look real close, I can see the future shadowed in them like a gypsy's crystal ball.

"Liza!" exclaims a booming voice from the kitchen behind me.

Someone kisses the top of my head and I spin around to see Tyler, Avery's ex-gang-banger buddy, bumbling off into the living room. I wipe my scalp with a sweater sleeve, terrified of the communal diseases that could be lurking in Tyler's saliva. Tyler's face looks like it's constantly buffering, I'm told it's been reconstructed over three times, and the way Ty's bouncing off of Ritalin, I'm scared half to death that he's gonna bash his face on the coffee table and we're gonna have to go for round four. Consequences come up to bite you fast around these parts, like the floor rushing up to hit your face.

"Liza, have I shown you my lil man yet?" Tyler asks in a proud voice. I look at him, concerned and flinching.

"Tyler, I'm not sure what type of innuendo that is supposed to be but I'd really rather not see any of that…" I say laughing uncomfortably.

"Nah! Jeesh, get your mind out of the gutter!" He tells me, pulling up a photograph of an ultrasound on his phone. "Ain't he handsome?"

I had forgotten that Tyler's baby mama was pregnant. She is four foot and eleven inches of angry, a white girl with a dreamcatcher badly tattooed down the stubbed length of her right arm. I remember her best for the black eyes she leaves across Tyler's already mutilated face. He's too nice to fight back and too dumb to duck. She is sixteen with a two-year-old and another on the way.

"He's beautiful," I say, cradling the phone he gives me like it's an actual infant in the palm of my hand. "Does this mean you and Chelsea are back together then?"

"Nope!" he says before slamming his ass into the couch. "she still hates my guts." My heart goes out to Tyler, always upbeat, smiling dumbly despite everything. I chalk it up to his multiple brain injuries. His baby mama didn't even let him in the room for the delivery of his first kid. His daughter took her first breath, and he sat outside smoking a joint, trying to forget all that he was missing. I am learning that all love is violent, some couples are just more upfront about it than others.

This is a meaner world than my college town. It's the world I grew up in, different state same shit. I got a scholarship now, my parents are proud of me now. I'm the kid that got out. They'd kill me if they knew I spent my nights with the same type of people they tried so desperately to ship me away from. But the college kids are really no smarter; they just have Mommy and Daddy a phone call away to bankroll their mistakes. I can't live in their training wheel world. I grew up on motorcycles.

Avery's buddies' parents either abandoned them, gave up on them, or offered them up to the foster care system long ago. These are the boxcar children all grown up, working to keep themselves in Ramen noodles and health insurance and booze. They are what the government calls your "throw away children," but that's the thing, you can't really "throw away" someone who already has a heartbeat. You can only forget them and hope they'll go away.

Tyler's freestyling to the stereo beats that are making the floor shake. Avery says that Ty could make it big, if he just got his own beats, but what Ty's spitting sounds like he's tripping over every other syllable.

"Liza's here and now we can go to the bar, or at least you Motherfuckahs can get in the car. Five days shy, gonna stay here and cry. Or maybe rub one, out right here on this futon," Ty spits.

"Not in *my* living room, you're not," Emmet, Avery's brother, protests from the kitchen. Emmet is nearly a fifth of Jack deep judging by the bottle in his gorilla sized fist and nothing much has changed. His mouth still marches on in the same stoic line. He likes to think he is the dad here. He always looks like an out of uniform cop. He never drinks, he's usually "too good" for that. I'm left wondering why tonight is any different.

Katrina and Ben are boxing in the living room, dangerously close to the windows and dangerously close to me. Ben recently broke up with his high school sweetheart. Katrina is his best bro, now his best fuck buddy. Nothing exclusive, he tells us, just someone to lay under while he gets over the love of his life. But I'm not sure how much I believe him. I see the way he looks at her; the way he looks at her face more than her tits. I don't think either of them really knows what kind of monster they've created here with this non-relationship. Katrina punches Ben in the hand and he screams.

"Jesus! I think you popped another stitch!" Ben says. He has nine stitches in his hand from punching a TV Wednesday night. The screen was already broken, his ex took a bat to it on his way out of the house. The stitches were in the name of anger management, all fun and games until the emergency room nurse is plucking plasma screen from your knuckles with tweezers at two am.

"Stop being such a pussy!" Katrina screams in Ben's face. She is two heads taller than him. If she really wanted to, she could end him. She doesn't really want to though. This is just for show, this is just all she knows about flirting, two eagles, talons intertwined, plummeting to the ground.

"Fuck this, this is stupid. I'm not gonna fight a girl," Ben surrenders.

Katrina's shirt is riding up to just underneath her bra line. Both her bra straps are drooping down her shoulders. She makes no move to adjust any of this but instead gestures emphatically to the rest of the room.

"C'mon, really? Is everyone too scared to fight me?"

"I'll do it!" Emmet says. His biceps are nearly the width of Katrina's skull. She may have met her match.

3....2.....1

Emmet has Katrina pinned against the wall in a matter of seconds, his hands swallowing up her wrists somewhere above her head.

"Say Uncle," he demands.

"Never," Katrina says. They lock eyes, neither of them flinching. For a moment I am terrified that their lips will lock too, then Ben will punch Emmet in the face and there will be a brawl for real. But they just stand there, with Katrina pinned beneath Emmet, the grey matter of possibility the only thing hanging between them.

Have you ever witnessed a car accident? Not the thralls of screeching metal and chrome peeling back like cadaver skin, but the minutes before. The seconds before, when you can still pinpoint when the driver should have applied the brakes or should have diverted the steering wheel. Experts say that the passenger seat is the most dangerous. You have all this advice built up in your head, but you can't do anything about it but go along for the ride.

"Last one to the truck has to buy me a beer!" Avery yells, bolting for the door. I shiver, hoping that everyone else is too drunk to see what I've seen.

"You're riding bitch!" I yell after Avery as we sprint to Emmet's two-door pick up.

"Go on guys, have fun, be safe," Ty calls after us. "I'll just be waiting here, jacking off on your couch."

***

Saturday night is always bar night, a short-skirted and shit-faced affair. Avery's friends, who don't have girls yet, are always scouring the waters, hunting for those 'other fish in the sea' they were promised when they broke it off with their last girl. The boys among us that have girls, like Avery, are always here to show us off, dangling us like lures in front of strangers and then threatening to kick any man's teeth in when they inevitably move too close, when they try to talk to us. We girls are possession and not mouthpiece. These nights are all tight nerves and hair pin trigger fists. Saturday night is nicotine laced excitement, is sloppy story material, is spotty memory terrifying. I'm never sure if we will make it home without a police record or without injury, and I call this fun because I don't really have any other word for it.

The bar is one I've never been to before. The boys had just moved to this small city, an hour away from my apartment. The move is turning out to be harder on me than I was expecting. Avery's transmission has blown in his Subaru. The car he is renting no longer has a windshield, mysteriously enough. It is November. This means that I either have to get Emmet to come pick me up or I have to drive. So basically it comes down to me driving, in the dark, praying that the GPS doesn't do that possessed thing where it lifts the avatar of my car off the road and informs me that my ass is underwater and that I should, "turn around when possible."

This bar is what I like to call an "adult bar." I am used to college bars where there is a trouble ceiling. How far can you go? Everyone around you lives in a dorm. Somebody grabs your ass, so what? They're all in your age range. No, not here, in this too small, wanna-be lumberjack bar where middle age men lick their teeth like wolves when I walk by. I'm only in my slip. I had to take my sweater off, it's too crowded in here. I have a stress rash in my armpit, so I can't wear deodorant right now. People are mistaking my self preservation against BO for flirting.

"If anyone touches you, I'll kick their ass," Avery tells me, even though Katrina's hand is already looped around *my* ass. Emmet and Ben are elbow to elbow with strangers at the bar, their backs to us. My back is to the drum set of the band that's supposed to show up anytime now. In the meantime, washed-up 90s grunge is pouring out of hidden speakers, reminding most of the patrons of their twenties. I'm reminded of when I was five, when *sex and candy* were just pretty words. Avery is adrift in the crowd, not at the bar, but not against the wall either. We are blocked in by strangers, and it's getting hard to breathe.

"Avery, you're lucky I don't steal Liza away from you," Katrina says. "I just absolutely love women."

I snuggle in closer to her as if to ask, *could you please? Steal me away, just for tonight and I promise your girl will make it worth your time.* Ben flicks a look back at Katrina from the bar. His eyes follow the trail of her arm around me and his mouth carves out that wolfy grin he has that makes it look like he's about to eat you up. Avery picks on Ben occasionally, telling him he looks like Jafar because he's from Pakistan. I'd agree, but not because of his homeland, but because he has this unshakable look of a Disney villain when he smiles.

"Take it up with her," Avery says. "I'm fine with it if she is."

Katrina stoops down so that her lips are at my ear. She whispers so that only I can hear.

"What do you think, Baby Girl? Can I fuck you?"

I don't have the nerve to say yes, but I nod my head against her arm and pray that she understands. My palms are sweating and my knees are shaking. I'm an awkward middle school boy at a dance. I'm fumbling to get my tongue unglued from the roof of my mouth. I take a long sip from my vodka lemonade, play with a cherry stem between my teeth. Avery watches me like I'm Atlas holding up the world, scared to look away, because maybe if he does, I might drop the ball.

***

Emmet leaves a dent in the car next to ours when he pulls his big two-door truck out of the lot. The truck barely makes a sound as it collides with the Toyota, crumpling in the door like a paper lunch bag. Emmet stops the truck to look at the damage, but he doesn't make a move to do anything about it.

"Yep, we're getting out of here," Emmet says, spinning the wheel. He is too drunk to drive, but we all can say the same. We are out of options, and we are out of the parking lot before the Toyota owner even knows what hit them.

"That door's not gonna open anymore," Ben says, not out of judgment but in wide-eyed

speculation. I'm wondering how Emmet can just walk out of this without any thought to the havoc he has just wreaked on someone else's life. I am wondering how the passengers of that car will ever make it home when they finally stumble out of the bar. I'm wondering if this is even a mistake they can afford to fix.

I stare at Emmet in the driver's seat. The truck is swerving slightly. I'm unconcerned; this truck is a tank, we will be fine. He's humming along to the mind-numbing country song that's blasting over the speakers like nothing had happened at all. *I was gonna be your forever, and you were gonna be my wife.* Katrina is riding bitch next to Emmett and Ben is in the passenger seat, one hand cast out at his side so that Katrina's palm can rest in it. Ben's got his drunken eyes lost in the street lights slipping past the window, so he doesn't see the way Katrina's thigh is lined up with Emmet's, the way her toe is tracing nonsense letters into the side of his calf.

Me and Avery are in the back seat, seat belts cast to the side so we can get even closer. I'm freezing, my hands shaking, my shoulders trembling like I've just seen a ghost. Or the future. Avery pulls his Carhartt jacket over my shoulders. He runs his hands up and down my fishnet-bound legs, down my arms, like someone warming their hands by a campfire.

"My Liza," he whispers, like it's some type of prayer. "My Liza." As if I had never and would never belong to anyone but him.

***

The bass is shaking the graveyard of bottles on the coffee table, and Tyler is snoring loud enough to match it. Ben runs in and flips Tyler off the couch. Tyler lays on the floor, unresponsive for a moment, pretending to be dead. Violence is a term of endearment for these boys; I no longer question it. I do, however, worry that one of the screws in Tyler's reconstructed face will bust loose.

"Jesus, Ty!" Emmet says. "What did I tell you about the bass?"

"What? Only neighbor you guys got is the graveyard next door," Ty says.

"Emmet's just scared we're gonna wake the dead," I comment. Emmet shoots me a dirty look. After cleaning my vomit off the stairs last weekend, he is in no mood for my sarcasm.

"Good one, baby girl," Katrina tells me, grabbing my hands. She leads me into what appears to be a waltz to a dubstep remix of a bad Halsey song. She pulls my arm up for me to spin her, but they don't reach that far. She stoops down to my level, crossing her hands over the back of my neck, resting her head on my shoulder as if we had always danced this way. As if we always would.

"I'm a wanderess, I'm a one night stand," she sings along. "Don't belong to no city, don't belong to no man....I'm your hurricane."

My heart is in my throat. All I can smell is her cheap perfume, all synthetic dahlias and it's eating up all the air left in the room. I can't feel the floor anymore beneath my stockinged feet. I am not drunk enough to be here.

I break away from Katrina and retreat to Avery's room upstairs to pour myself a drink. Avery follows me up. He hugs me from behind in front of his bedroom mirror. I look at this relationship status picture of us in the looking glass. I like how easy this looks, when we're together like this. *This is what you've always wanted,* I think to myself, I remind myself. Avery bites my shoulder. He doesn't love bite, even though that's surely what he means to do. He bites like he wants to tear off a chunk of me to keep as his own. It hurts, but I never mind. I display his teeth marks like butterflies caught in amber. A proof of something beautiful and fleeting. *Someone loves me enough to leave their mark on me.* That's how I used to see it, anyway. But now I'm just reminded of a dog marking its territory and I struggle not to shudder against the confines of his arms.

"If you guys fuck, I get to watch, right?" Avery asks me. I'm facing away from the mirror now with a vodka bottle in my hand, so he can't see the look of disgust creeping over my face. He doesn't understand why the question he just asked is so wrong. He doesn't get why it is warped that he asked to watch me cheat on him. Because it is with a woman, it is entertainment, not betrayal in his eyes, but from where I'm standing, it is no different. But I can't critique this out loud, terrified that this is conditional, and this hall pass he has granted me only plays by his rules.

I spin around and kiss him, as long and deep as my swig from the vodka bottle.

"Sure thing babe," I say, my lips forming the letters against his. The words are venom in my teeth, slowly killing me, but I don't have the guts to argue. I spin on my heels and head back downstairs, bracing myself for whatever comes next.

The stairs are too steep and the railing is dangling by a single screw. I'm trying not to trip because I'm feeling my vodka more than I should. Avery said, when he was moving in, he saw the shadow of a little girl tumbling down the stairs. He says that when no one is home, he can sometimes hear this ghost girl's laughter echoing from the halls. This is the spirit that makes me terrified to walk downstairs to the bathroom alone at night. But now, tripping over my own toes, I wonder if it wasn't a premonition. I wonder if that clumsy ghost was not a future me, falling to my death on the stained carpet below. Avery takes my hand and walks beside me, and I think that he is worried about the same thing.

There's only Tyler in the living room. There's a silence heavy as the blanket of snow outside, weighing down the room underneath the bumping of bad rap music playing over the flat screen. It's some video with a guy with ketchup-red braids singing about broccoli, but not really about vegetables at all. The boys only listen to songs about money, bitches, drugs, a prosperity they will never know. A world they think they can reach with low grade cocaine and empty Domino's pizza boxes. But our world will never be like the videos; this is rural Maine, not Compton.

"Where'd everybody go?" Avery asks. I can hear the recoil of a headboard hitting the wall like the click of a trigger, or the clacking of fenders in the background. My head is buzzing too loud to know if the sounds are coming from Ben or Emmet's room. *For the love of God, let it be Ben's room.*

"Well, Emmet's fucking Ben's girl," Tyler says in his dopey way, as if he is buffered from the consequences of this. He summarizes like it's something he's seen on TV and not something that's threatening to blow the whole house down. "Ben went for a walk so he doesn't kill him."

I can picture Ben walking in the snow, a cigarette in one hand and his other hand balled into a fist deep in his pocket. Ben has gotten arrested for lesser reasons. He is possessive, he is vindictive. He has lost everything in the past month; the love of his life, his house, even his dog. Katrina is not the great love of his life, he does not even love her, but she is all he has. In his mind, she is all he owns, and he will defend that to the death,

"What?" Avery says, sprinting in front of me. He turns the corner to Emmet's room, like he still has time to stop this, like he still has time to save this fragile family we have strung together with joints and beer cans. I can hear the thud of his fist against the door, and I know that Avery is pretending the wood is Emmet's face. I pull myself up to sit on the unlit surface of the stove top in the kitchen. I hug the ripped fishnets of my knees into my chest. I'm crying and I don't know why.

"What have you done?" Avery shouts in a voice that seems out of place on his goofy face. "What have you done?"

***

Ben, Avery, and I are upstairs in Ben's room. Avery having gone after Ben and fished him out of the night before he caught frostbite on his clenched fists, before Ben had enough time to come up with too many bad ideas out there in the midnight cold. A big screen TV is playing Kanye's "Power." Avery and Ben are swapping around a joint and staring at the tiny Kanye on the screen as if he's Jesus Christ, like his words are gonna save them. Me and Avery are sitting on the futon that serves as Ben's bed. I'm holding Avery's hand, tracing the scabs that have formed over his knuckles, from the door, from other fights. I can read his hands just like a fortune teller; I can tell you exactly where he's been.

Ben is pacing the floor with a wooden bat clenched in his fists. The bat is painted with specks of blood so old it looks like dried nail polish. It's part of an ongoing investigation, the investigation being that Ben hit a man twice in the head and once in the chest with the bat. He brags now that the man is no longer smart enough to fuck with him. I think he's considering doing the same to Emmet, who's asleep downstairs.

"It's not worth it, put it down," I tell him.

"Probation," Avery reminds him. *My brother,* I think he should have said, but he leaves Emmet out of the conversation.

Ben looks surprised and stares at his hands as if wondering how the bat got there in the first place. He drops it as if it were about to bite him.

Tyler is asleep on the couch downstairs. Katrina's in the shower. The rest of us are listening to Ben make promises he can't keep about Katrina.

"She can get her own ride home tomorrow, I'm done," he says for maybe the seventh time.

"You'd never see this happening to us," Avery says, squeezing the ball of my knee. "I take relationships seriously."

As if to prove him wrong, Katrina appears in the doorway wearing nothing but a towel. Ben's got murder in his eyes, but Katrina talks before anything else can be said.

"Tyler's peeing on the stairs."

"Ty! What the fuck man?" the boys are yelling, tumbling down the stairs after each other to throw Tyler's ass out in the snow.

Katrina takes a seat on the futon next to me. Her towel is barely long enough to cover everything it needs to. I stare at the rappers jumping around on the TV and pretend not to notice. She leans her head on my shoulder.

"Baby girl, I'm single as fuck," she says.

"I know," I say. "Ben has no right to be mad about this."

"Do you think I'm a bad person?" She asks. I loop my arm around her bare shoulder. She's a foot taller than me, but she looks so small.

"No, you're wonderful," I tell her.

"At least you got a boyfriend," she says. "Me, I don't got nothing. Baby girl, I'm single as fuck."

I look down at where her thigh matches up with mine. At where her fist is dropped in her lap. There is a bracelet of bruises wrapped around her wrist. I know it's not from the bar fights; if it were she would have displayed it as if it were something from Tiffany's. It's not from her fling with Emmet, it's a shade of yellow that's too old for that. It's a cuff about the size of Ben's fist. I trace the edge of it with a fingertip. She pulls it away as if my fingernails are made of lit cigarettes.

I have a sudden urge to punch her too. To bring back that girl I saw in the living room earlier. The girl that threatened to fight any boy that dared mess with her. I want to bring back the girl that promised to fuck me on my boyfriend's kitchen table. That girl that didn't need anybody, but wanted everybody. *Where is that girl?* The girl that made me want to be louder, to stand taller. Had it all been an act? Was Katrina really no bigger than this sobbing mess resting her cheek on my shoulder? I kiss her on the cheek, trying to soak up the tears trailing down her face. She pulls her lips up to meet mine. She tastes like Jack Daniel's and stale cigarettes and the mucus of crying over senseless things.

"You'll really do it for anybody," Ben says. We fling apart. Ben is standing in the doorway, staring at Katrina as if she's dog shit on his shoe.

She flips him off, grabs the back of my head and kisses me so violently I can taste her blood between my teeth. She pulls away, and pats me on the head.

"Good night baby girl," she says, walking out of the room and out of my life for what I assume will be forever. Ben will break it off with her. She's not Emmet's type. Sober Emmet is "better" than the likes of her. She'll find another house, another gaggle of boys to fall in love with her, because who wouldn't?

"I can't believe she had the nerve to come in here in a towel," Ben says, when all the boys are back, assembled around the TV once more.

She doesn't belong to you. I want to tell him. *Your heart is not hers to break.* I want to tell him she can do what she wants, with a mouth that is still rimmed with her lip gloss.

But Avery sits down next to me and bites my shoulder.

"I saw tonight working out a whole lot better," I say instead.

"Me too," Avery says. "But Tyler pissed all over Emmet's sweatshirt."

"I'm gonna have to buy that man a beer and start calling him Karma," Ben says, showing off his first smile in hours.

The boys watch J. Cole sing about the difference between sisters and hoes and a girl you shouldn't save because she doesn't want to be. There is no movement but the passing of a joint occasionally, no sound but the sputtered coughs of smoke going down the wrong pipe.

***

Avery and I are watching *Sons of Anarchy* in his room, a half bare mattress and a floor littered with Twisted Tea cans at varying states of fullness. We lie facing each other, hands wrapped about the other's arm, like two mummies trying to fit into the same sarcophagus. He's tracing infinity signs into my shoulder. He kisses my forehead, my nose, my lips. I'm missing when this was enough.

"I'm so happy we're just simple," he tells me, before sticking his tongue in my mouth. His hands fumble for the elastic band of my fishnets. I blindly unbuckle his belt. This is a dance we've mastered now, the choreography identical every time, as precise as a Broadway performance. Two years from now with an engagement ring on my finger, five years from now with a baby asleep in the next room, thirty years from now when we're mapping the geography of middle age together, come find me. I'll be right where I am now, on top of him, while he cradles the back of my skull and calls me his "good girl."

This is what you've always wanted? I think again, but now there is a question mark that I can't shake. The mattress creaks beneath us in a steady rhythm like the tattoo of a spring shower.

I keep my eyes battened shut though. I'm too busy thinking of other storms. Tonight doubts are falling like rain in the drought of this bedroom. *What have I done?*

How to Leave

It is a Wednesday night. Christmas time, but the tequila on your breath makes it feel like the Day of the Dead. You have snuck out of Margarita night early. You see no need to go to the bar anymore, you have found your person, there is nothing you can do intoxicated in public now that would not be done better at home, in your room, in your bed.

You trace the nonsense lines of your boyfriend's tattoo sleeve with a blood red fingernail. This bed, that so many others had bombed into a battlefield, had barb-wired into a no man's land, is now a ticker-tape parade homecoming. He kisses the cigarette burn that some other lover before him had left on the inside of your elbow as if he could sew up all your scars with his lips. For a moment you think maybe he can. You wonder if time could repay you now, stop for a little while, just so you could spend a few years learning happy, doing nothing but listening to each other's heartbeats. Avery and you have good days and you have bad days. It's been a good day ever since you came back from Thanksgiving, enough time to suffocate your doubts.

"You could stay forever, if you want, you know," your boyfriend tells you. For a moment you consider it. You can see a local teaching job, a modest house, a couple of school lunches packed on an early morning kitchen table. For a moment your feet consider what it would be like to do something other than run. You catch your breath for what feels like the first time in years.

But then you see the drafts, stacked in piles around your mattress.

Times New Roman font with red pen comments scribbled across the pages for revision. Stories of other boys, tales of all the ways you have tried to avenge yourself since then. What happens if the essays stay there, on the floor, forever? If their pages fade into nothing but carpet? What happens if no one ever sees these but you? Could you live with that?

You think of last Thursday, your Senior reading. You remember a podium, a microphone, your knees shaking like they were trying to break out of your skin. You read for an audience for the first time, a broken glass and heart strained story about pretty heartbreak and violent love. Your tongue felt too big for your mouth. You kept tripping over words that you'd heard in your dreams. You were trying not to choke up with Matt, Alex and Dio's names in your teeth. This story seems to be about a different girl now. You were feeling foolish for believing that you could make this audience feel for these people the way that you once felt for them. Your writing and your introduction at that reading proclaimed that you have no idea what you want to do with your life. You are a Senior with no future. You had never expected to live this long, so you have no plan for whatever comes next.

After, your professor had said you should think about a Master's degree. Strangers from the audience called all the ugly in your scrap metal words beautiful. "I like to try to get a gauge of who the writer is from their writing, when you were up there, all I could think was, this girl is fearless," a underclassmen with grandfather glasses and a crop top told you. And it meant more than all the "beautifuls" you've collected in your entire life. And for once this writing business of yours seemed like something more than what you had always assumed it was; something more than dancing with corpses with a pen in your hand. The future had stopped seeming so much like a drop off, a dead end. You looked out across the horizon of what was left of your twenties and could see pavement there. You had places to go, places you could go.

Back in your bed, you look at Avery, this riot toothed man beside you. You bargain with yourself in your head. Would you trade your voice for his arms? Would you trade your tongue for his lips? Would you trade your words for his half hung promises? You already have your answer when you kiss him and tell him that forever is a long time. You don't have the heart to tell him no. You've never had the heart to tell anybody no.

You will wake up at four am the next morning screaming from the mouth of a nightmare. In the dream, there had been a baby in a jumper at the corner of your bed. She had been crying, her face accusatory and candy apple red. You scooped her up and took her for a walk outside, because being outside had always pacified you as an infant. You were walking her through the trailer park that is your neighborhood. You had enough time to consider that you wanted a better life for your child than the Marlboro moms and weed dads outside your apartment door.

Then the quiet broke, a pack of porcupines, rabid and mean were at your tail. You ran in a flurry of snarling teeth and flying quills. You tucked the baby in your flannel shirt and took off running, catching quills between your toes. All you could smell was your own blood, copper laced and all too familiar, but you kept running.

By the time you reached your fire escape, the baby had five quills stuck through her heart, her head and limbs had fallen off. You were just holding an empty shell of a body, for dear life. You had tried your best, but there was nothing left to save. Avery was sitting on the fire escape, a joint tucked between his fingers. His face was placid, calm in the wake of your panic. "It's ok babe," he told you in the nightmare. "She always cried too much anyway."

You wake Avery up with your crying. He kisses the tears away from your cheeks. Collects the eyeliner that is bleeding down your face. "It's ok babe," he assures you. "It wasn't real. It was only a nightmare." But you are not sure where that line is drawn anymore.

The next morning before you leave for vacation, Avery will give you a gift card to Til Death tattoo for Christmas. You will stop there on your way home for break. You are determined to get *for the story* in gothic font scrawled across your upper thigh. Like a garter a bride would wear on her wedding day. Everything you have ever done has been in the name of a story. Everything that you are going to do from this day on, is in the name of your stories. You are married to this in ink and in your word. It is a promise more than skin deep. The words are intricate, each letter as unique as a thumbprint, as delicate as an eyelash. Your tattoo artist, Steve, a stout man with a bundle of burning sage tattooed on his calf muscle tells you he is not sure he can do it, but he'll try. That's really all you ask of anybody anymore.

Sitting in the waiting room alone, you glance at the empty space on the leather couch next to you and remember Alex sitting in Matt's lap. You snap them both, say "guess where I am?" They will not respond; they have class today. You always take it too personally when people have lives outside of their interactions with you. This is one of those times.

Mexican sugar skulls smile at you from the shelves. You absentmindedly wish that we could all be as transparent and beautiful. A pin up drawing of an African American woman with an afro made up of tentacles smiles coyly from the wall, a banner with the word "Octopussy" bundled at her feet. Matt always joked that this would be his next tattoo. You have a half-assed belief that lifetime commitments should be a serious consideration not made on humor or whims.

You are flipping through the waiver, four pages that you could recite by heart by now. You breeze through each question, sure and bored. Until you get to, *I am not pregnant or nursing.*

A fear that feels a lot like the crown of thorns drawing on the brick wall in front of you grips your heart. You can no longer remember the last time you had your period. You start counting off on your fingers. 4, 5, 6… 8 weeks late.

Your palms sweat into the papers in your hands. You bite your lip, pinch your thigh, try to convince yourself that this revelation is a bad dream. You sign your name by this section, regardless. With your signature declaring otherwise, it cannot possibly be true. You walk back to the front desk, slide the packet of your written consent back to Steve. He looks at you, eyes concerned and magnified through his hipster style glasses. You look at him with fresh eyes. Your tattoo artist has been the only consistent man in your life for the better part of two years now. And you don't know if this is sad or bad ass but you feel like crying. "Wow, I don't think I've ever seen you nervous before," he says. "It's just your leg, it won't be that bad."

"I know," you tell him, trying to play at a smile. Your leg is nothing. Your life, on the other hand…

Frida Kahlo's Guide to Painting

"I hope you get the answer you're looking for, ma'am," the Walmart cashier, a world weary elderly lady with a can't be bothered pixie cut, tells me. I swipe my card through and wish silently to myself that the Walmart of my college town had self check out. The one back home did, but home was no place for this kind of purchase. Christmas break was worry, silence, a crash course in forgetting. I am too anxious, too tired to speak this morning. And I can't take the sound of pity in this woman's voice.

"Thank you," I squeak out, as if I had asked for this. My hands are shaking trying to loop my fingers around the plastic checkout bag. It contains a lemon-lime Powerade, a Monster, blood red OPI nail polish and my first pregnancy test. I bolt for the automatic doors. The greeter, a smiling girl in a wheelchair tells me to, "have a nice day ma'am." I spend my walk to the car, through the slush laden parking lot, listing all the reasons why this will not be the case today.

This is my defining moment. From this day forth, all Walmart employees in my college town will refer to me as *ma'am*. The title will catch like wildfire from blue vest to blue vest. It's like they had a staff meeting about me. *Attention employees, this is no mere girl in your checkout line. Oh, No! This lady has seen some shit.*

Or maybe I'm making myself up to be more important than I actually am. This is my key character flaw. I mean nothing to nobody, and here I sit at the center of the universe watching it spin round my feet.

***

Once upon a time, there lived a little girl who dreamed of becoming a doctor. She had once had polio and she wanted to help other children from the same fate. The girl's name was Frida Kahlo and she never did make it to medical school. She was a mischievous thing, joining up with a group of rebel students at her private school, who sought to prove their points by any means necessary, sometimes blowing out windows with firecrackers. Frida would always claim that her first memory was the sound of bullets whizzing by her childhood home in the throes of the revolution. War was in Frida's blood; she was raised on it.

It was this school, this bone deep rebellion, that brought her path to cross with that of Diego Rivera. He was painting a mural in her school's auditorium. It was love at first sight. "I will marry that man someday," she said to Alejandro, her then boyfriend, and for better or worse, she would.

Diego was not a handsome man. "My toad," she called him, with the amount of affection given to words like *Darling* or *baby*. Toad. Despite his ugliness, Diego never slept alone, and what others would see as warning, Frida painted as challenge.

Frida's parents never understood what she saw in Diego. In her twenties, their little girl had already been broken in more ways than they could have ever imagined possible for her. The polio, a trolley accident that had left her sprawling on the pavement, encrusted in gold like some fallen angel, a pole piercing through all her holy places. Keeping Frida alive had become expensive. Every parent believes that they will not stoop to sell their daughter to the highest bidder, but sometimes, there really is no other choice. And she had said she was in love, after all.

Her mother called it the marriage of "an elephant to a dove." Her daughter, all 98 pounds of hellfire stood awkwardly next to this billowing, middle aged man, who seemed to think it fashionable to hoist his pants up to his armpits. Her daughter was so beautiful, how could this have happened? "You can do so much better," she told Frida. Her mother did not attend the wedding. She called it blasphemy to go to church for something you didn't believe in.

Her father was more open minded. He pulled Diego aside in an attempt to warn him. "Are you sure about this?" he asked him. "She's the devil, you know." Diego shrugged his shoulders and the marriage went on as planned. Or at least the ceremony did.

***

It is Christmas break, and I am sitting at my best friend's kitchen table staring at my hands in my lap because looking anywhere else in this room makes me want to cry. I think about the beginnings of fingernails, buried way down deep in the soil of my cuticles. I think about all the things we cannot see, but that have been there evidently all along, the raw ingredients an inevitable fate just waiting for their chance to break the surface. And yet, if you were to look at your hands now, everything would be completely still.

My best friend, Lane, took a nannying job in Florida last October. She lived with a wealthy lady and her daughter, residing in the apartment above their garage. She got horrible, delightful sunburns; her Irish skin was never meant for any place more tropical than the streets of New Haven.

She met a boy that lived on a sailboat. His last name was Kelley, and we gushed at how this must be fate, because of our childhood obsession with Christian Bale's *Newsies* character, Jack Kelly. He had a smiley face stick and poke tattooed on his ass. Lane would send me snapchats of this in the early morning, when the sun was just coming up over the Florida coast. Her life was an adventure beyond my understanding. Her life was happy, her life was loved.

I woke up in August to a text message from her saying she was going to have a baby in September. I rubbed my eyes, thinking they had failed me. I pinched myself. I wanted to scream for her, but I was sitting in a summer camp cabin, supervising other people's children, that I hoped would turn out better than we had. Instead I just typed back, "Are you ok?"

"I never wanted kids," she confessed to me. "But this is my life now, so I suppose I should get on with it."

"What are you going to do?" I asked.

She didn't have the heart to get rid of it. She never mentioned the father, this had nothing to do with him now. Lane packed up her independence and moved back into her parents' house in Connecticut, half a country away from the life she had lived. She no longer spoke about sailboats or apartments above the garage or stick and poke tattoos in inappropriate places. The Lane that had lived in Florida had died. I never heard from that part of her ever again.

***

I don't feel up to dealing with any more people today, but I pull into Dunkin Donuts anyway. Coffee is a diuretic and I need to produce a lot of urine in a very small amount of time. It is a month from Valentine's Day and the store is decked out in pink and red. Glossy streamers dangle from the ceiling. I cannot help but compare them to some bad Frida Kahlo painting, all misplaced organs and ribbons. Every donut is heart shaped, and it is more optimistic than I can take. Love is a holiday that I never seem to end up celebrating.

The cashier looks startled by the look on my face, which I can only assume is something of the funeral variety. He smiles so wide he looks like a lobotomy victim to compensate for my disposition.

"Smile, it's Saturday!" he offers. The guy isn't bad looking, with chocolate brown eyes and some tasteful tattoo sleeves., but at the very core of him he resembles my potential baby daddy a little too much for me to bear. I wince visibly and order coffee, black with ice. He will write his number in sharpie on my cup. I will throw it out after I'm done. It's not personal, it's just what I do with good intentions.

***

Frida quickly realized that she had bitten off more than she could chew. Diego had a habit of spiting their marriage by openly denouncing monogamy. Frida was beginning to understand that love was just a four letter word. She was beginning to understand that a marriage certificate is just a piece of paper, flimsy and easily torn. Frida would say later that she never really had Diego, not *really*. Diego loved his work, and then maybe Frida was a close second. Frida loved Diego before all else, she proclaimed to anyone that would listen, that she would give her life for him. But she had to be able to keep him for any of those pretty words to mean anything at all. What Frida needed was stability. What Frida needed was a family, a child.

It is the cruelest of realities in this world that sometimes the things that are impossible for us are sometimes the things that we want most. The trolley accident never left Frida. Death trailed her as a loyal lover since that day, his bony fingers and toothy grin peering up at her from the foot of her and Diego's marriage bed. He wanted to remind her that she had married *him* first and would forever belong to him before she ever belonged to Diego. The accident had shifted too much in Frida, her bones, her organs, her soul, her life. Friends would say that after "the incident," in all the years that she had left to her, they really were just watching Frida die. But she still had a stupid hope that something would rise from the ashes. Frida got pregnant once, twice, three times, each ending in a medically necessary abortion. Frida's body was no home, why should Diego have any interest in living there?

Diego went on tour for his artwork, the cities of America, a country Frida did not understand, a land where inside gentlemen ate off golden plates, while outside bums begged on the street corners. In this strange land of disparity, Frida found herself pregnant once again. Access to abortion was a country away; it was time to sink or swim. She nearly drowned.

Frida miscarried, blood blooming through her traditional skirts like a flower in one of her paintings. She was admitted to a New York hospital, a place that didn't understand her or her language. Death smiled up at her from between the guardrails of her bed, his lipless mouth taunting an "I told you so." She spit in his face, screamed at him to leave her be.

She was a ghost of herself in a plain hospital shift. Diego had to blink to recognize her, Frida had never looked weak anywhere else but here. She was pounds lighter without her jewelry, the shackles she wore like an Aztec Queen and now she threatened to float up off the earth entirely without all that gold to weigh her down.

Diego had fallen in love with a woman who was the embodiment of Mexico and everything it meant for him. Here, she looked too girl, too human. Her golden capped incisors flashed like fangs through the industrial lighting as the last remnant of the person, the country, he had married. She was all that she could give him, she could not give him a son, she could not give him a future. She knew better than to believe she would be enough.

***

Lane tells me that the baby has a habit of scratching his face while he's sleeping. He'll wake up with claw marks all across his cheeks like he's been sleeping with wolves. She can never seem to cut his nails short enough to keep him from harm, no matter how hard she tries.

My own face hurts from trying to keep up a smile. I honestly don't know what other facial expression is acceptable for going to visit your best friend's new, accident baby. I am sitting in her parents' kitchen. The same kitchen where we would secretly mix up brownie batter in the dead of night as children, stifling our giggles as not to wake her mother, a dragon and ginger woman. We'd drink the batter until we felt sick, then quickly try to hide the evidence, disposing the excess in toilets that would inevitably clog and sinks whose drains would bubble up sugar for weeks after. My heart breaks for what devious girls, smart, mischievous little girls grow into. We'd spent most of our childhoods trying to see what we could get away with, we grew up to realize that the answer was nothing at all.

I'm biting my tongue, holding in the questions I want to ask her: *who's the baby's daddy? When are you gonna move out? What happened, Lanie? Are you happy?* She can't answer these questions any better than I can, so we talk circles around the elephant in the room. I want to tell her that the baby looks nothing like her, there is not a freckle that dots this child's face, no stray star of resemblance to light the way. His hair sticks in tufts to his scalp, all cornsilk and no copper. She is holding a stranger, but you can't tell a mother this.

We talk about the baby's future, what incredible things he is learning to do with his feet. We do not talk about Florida. We do not talk about the math I did in the tattoo parlor waiting room. There's no use asking questions that no one has answers for.

***

A half hour, one Powerade, a medium coffee and 20 fl oz of water later, I'm trying to piss on a stick the width of my pinky finger in the bathroom of my apartment. Which, for those alien to this feat, is a little bit like trying to land a jet plane on a french fry, tedious and death defying.

Time is ticking. My runner roommates have all been chugging their weight in water to prepare for today's race. We only have this one bathroom, so I gotta do this quick. I've never been this nervous to take a piss in my entire life.

And maybe, the devil on my shoulder admits, I'm avoiding something. As long as the test stays dry it's just a question mark, no plus or minuses involved. The part of me that got me into this mess in the first place whispers with all the sultriness of a speakeasy crooner, *Why do this now? Maybe you're just running late? No rush...*

There is frost icing the bathroom window. The sink is clogged, a fist sized clump of my roommate's hair sitting heavy in the pipes. The water drips, keeping time for me, like I am a contestant on *Jeopardy,* reminding me that I have to cough up an answer soon. The sink will overfill one day, a leaky faucet and a clogged drain are an equation for disaster. Not everything I ignore will go away, not in this house, not in this relationship, and especially not in this body.

***

Stripped down in a backless hospital shift, Frida could have been mistaken for any other woman on the planet. Her armor taken, her baby killed, she peered through the bed rails like a creature caged.

"He came out in pieces!" she screeched in Spanish at the nurses with the intensity and insanity of a mother bird flapping over a nest dashed on the sidewalk. The hospital personnel wasn't sure what to do with her, was afraid of her, this bruja with searing eyes and pointed golden teeth. She demanded they give her medical textbooks, diagrams, her child. They had no choice but to give in to Frida's demands or else become a sacrifice for this fallen Azteca Queen. The nurses justified their actions, maybe she would create art. Maybe all this morbidity would be to some end, some kind of good. They returned her son to her, in a jar.

***

Lane puts socks on the baby's hands while he sleeps. I think of Native American babies strapped to backboards, their mothers leaving these makeshift cribs to hang from trees like nooses in the midday sun.

I think of the way Lane used to wrap her sleeves around her hands until she had worn thumb holes into all of her sweatshirts when we were children. She didn't want to see her wrists. She was always terrified of blood even though all she read were vampire novels. Her mother would yell at her, would tell her to put her hands where she could see them. How else would Lane be able to catch herself if she fell?

I think of Lane now, working a waitressing job. I think of Lane swallowing her pride and moving back into her parents' house. I think of Lane watching Netflix while the baby sleeps, the voices of actors echoing off the walls of an empty midday house.

But for now, there is no lonely. For now we can pretend we are just hanging out like we used to. Nothing has changed except for the baby blinking in Lane's arms. He looks up, startled and disappointed to see that he is a part of the outside world. Lane kisses his cheek. It's a simple act, but the baby stares up at her as if she were God. Lane speaks to him as though he were an adult, rocking him back and forth saying, "We're never going back to Florida, no, we're not. All they have there is gym rats and beach bums and cocaine"

"Lane!" I exclaim through laughter.

"He's too young to understand," She justifies. "thank God."

And I think she is talking about more than just the warped little nursery rhyme she has recited for him. What will she tell him of his story? Anything? What history do you write for a child whose beginning is something you vow never to go back to? Whose beginning is something you spend the rest of your life learning to forget?

***

I balance the test on the counter, wash my hands because my aim is less than perfect. I pull up the stopwatch on my IPod and wait, watching the windows in the test anxiously for the shadow of a doubt, or rather the outline of a second line. Two minutes doesn't seem like a long time, but it's given me too much time to think. I'm still trapped in our apartment bathroom. The numbers on my stopwatch are not flipping by fast enough. I consider leaving the room and coming back for it, but I'll be damned if someone like my roommate's boyfriend sees the results before me. It's bad enough the entire apartment already knows what I'm doing this morning. Telling them was the only way to justify the slightly suicidal look in my eye as I drove off to Walmart.

I am caught remembering a night from last fall, when staying over at Avery's was still a novelty and not a lifestyle choice. I woke screaming from a nightmare, in which I was paddling a kayak across a harbor. The sea was calm and the sky was the type of blue you only see in Pixar movies, cloudless and strikingly blue. A baby was perched on the tapering nose of the kayak. If I tried to reach for the infant, the boat would tip, drowning her. The best I could do was paddle to shore as quickly, as steadily as possible with a prayer in my teeth.

A lobster boat, all clanking cages and swearing men passed us, sprouting a wake. A wave, rolled up beneath the floor of the kayak, dislodging the child and tossing her into the surf. In the dream, I dove in after her, swam down deep until my eyes filled with dark and my lungs filled with ocean. I stretched my arms out as far as I could until I heard tendons popping loose from their fastenings. I dove until my teeth ached from the pressure and I feared my skull would pop like a zit under the weight of the water pressing down on it. I strained to see stubbed and chubby fingers in the blackness. I never found her.

Avery rocked me then, like the baby I had been trying to save in my sleep. I explained the nightmare to him and he reassured me, "Darlin, it's ok, we will never have to worry about a baby. We will never have a baby."

Now I know that Avery has jinxed us. Now I know the dream was premonition, the future reaching back to find me, warn me that I wouldn't be ready for whatever came next. I am not ready. I am seasick standing in the bathroom. Waiting.

I consider the two ways this could go, because the future has unlimited paths but we as humans are fond of limiting ourselves to forks in the road. It's simpler this way, to keep things Robert Frost. If the test is positive, I tell Avery and wait for the world to fall into place around me, whatever that looks like. If it's negative, I am saved. I can finish my education. The trailer park will not loom so heavy in my bedroom window. I will be free.

***

Diego found Frida in the hospital, unibrow scrunched in concentration over a sketch pad. The pieces of her son in his jar balanced on a table before her. She barely noticed Diego's entrance, scribbling frantically, trying to record this nearly perfect combination of her and Diego before the earth took their baby back as its own. She wanted to save this small shred of evidence that Diego had loved her at all, that this man with his big ideas for the future of Mexico, had chosen to make a future with her. But no matter how accurately she recorded this baby in a bottle, it did not matter. The family she had hoped for lay in pieces.

Frida did not return the jar, she would sleep with it in her night stand for the rest of her life, her tiny little family bobbing in formaldehyde, a tiny body curled and hopeless in spent possibility. This moment would never leave her. Death would never leave her. In the small hours of the morning, Death would lay his bony fingers across the fragile fabric of her shoulders, tell her how proud he was of her. She had finally given him a son.

***

Lane's coffee is going cold, untouched in the mug on the table. Her hands are full with the sprawling, smiling infant. He looks like love, he looks like purpose, like future.

"I kinda want one," I say without thinking. I jump at my own words. This is not as shocking as *I might have one,* but the sentence is still unexpected and out of place on my lips and it startles me. The syllables smack Lane in the face. She shoots me a look so frightened, you would have thought that I'd just chucked the baby like a football across the kitchen. In one moment, Lane's months of happily posting pictures of the baby, and bragging about her little man slip away. The curtain is pulled back, and I can see the regret and uncertainty that is actually running the show. Lanie looks so small, and I want to hug her. I want to reassure her that she is a person still, and not just a cautionary tale. Her hair hardly looks brushed and sticks out in autumn colored tufts from the ponytail she's scraped together. Her face, freckle dotted and frowning now is makeup free, her signature smoky eye look abandoned in the hustle of her new routine. The baby starts crying. His sock covered fists waving angrily like a victorious boxer. There is no silence left for my words.

***

Two minutes are up. I stare at the counter as if it's about to bite me. The test shows two parallel lines. I pick it up, cautious as a snake charmer. When I read it, it spells out *I told you so,* in a voice that sounds exactly like my mother's. I shake it back and forth in my palms, hoping this is some mistake, hoping that if I tilt it like an hourglass, it could give me more time. A few months, a year, a decade. But the lines stand stagnant, squinted eyed and mean staring up at me.

I can feel my knees buckling beneath the weight of this. I no longer have the strength to pull myself off the bathroom floor. The faucet drips, a roommate knocks on the door. The sound is too much. I don't respond. There are no words for this brand of millstone, for this kind of choke throated hope. My thoughts are running in a language they wouldn't understand and I'm too tired to explain. I tuck my knees up into my aching chest, trying to make myself as small and silent as I can. If I just sit here, will the world go on without me? I just want a minute, an hour, a lifetime to catch my breath.

***

Frida proclaimed that life was killing her. She put a razor to her scalp and let her raven hair fall in shards to the ground like the feathers of some wounded bird of paradise. She abandoned her skirts for suits, lynched neckties around her throat, trying her best to murder whatever in her still looked like mother.

Diego continued his affairs. He slept with Frida's sister, placing a final nail in the coffin. Frida had her own affairs, Leon Trotsky, Josephine Baker, Georgia O'Neil. Diego allowed her to sleep with women, but another man in her bed had him reaching for his pistol. They tried their hands at divorce.

But Frida was growing tired, homesick. Her bones were slowly dissolving in on themselves, she awoke each morning to find herself more fragile and broken than she used to be. Death was growing bolder now. His smiling mouth kissed the nape of her neck and was starting to whisper sweet nothings about his plans for their future together. So when Diego asked her to marry him again, she accepted, she offered him penance for every transgression. She would still die for him, she justified, he was, and always had been the only love of her life. Even if she wasn't his.

Frida died on morphine. Frida died ready. Frida died with Diego by her side. Frida died with her son in a jar, in the night stand by her bedside. She died with Death holding her hand and welcoming her home. The whole family was together, in the end, as she had always dreamed they would be.

***

"I mean like, some day," I sputter, trying to revise the horrible misunderstanding I have just spat up on Lane's kitchen table. Lane laughs, uncomfortably, her freckles dancing the way they do when she smiles. She knows that I'm making this up as I go along. We both play pretend in our own ways, it's the only way to survive. Lanie has enough of her own problems, I don't need to give her mine.

She paces the kitchen with the crying baby, trying to lure him back into sleep with the movement of her feet. I think of zoo tigers, circling the confines of their cages. I can't look at Lane anymore. I stare down at my hands, willing the revelation I've just presented back into the beds of my cuticles, pushing it out of sight and out of mind.

***

I stare at the bathroom ceiling until the house goes silent, until I am sure my roommates have left me behind. I stare at the ceiling until it turns to bloody sunset, until it fades to inky black. I grasp at straws, trying to think of a next step, a reason to stand up, a place to walk to. I don't know who to call, I don't know what to feel besides this empty, besides this heavy, besides this ending to whatever my life had been this morning. I just sit and stare at the test in my hand, wondering if I stay still long enough if I can become a fixture in this bathroom, as timeless and unchanging and unfeeling as the bathtub or the toilet. I wait for my limbs to freeze into porcelain, but of course this never happens. Only when I can no longer see the test in my fist for lack of daylight, do I start to cry.

How to Answer

You scrape yourself off the bathroom floor. You go out into the deserted kitchen. You sit on the floor beside the heater and try to warm your aching bones. You text your friend, Mercy, to tell her the unthinkable has happened. You swear her to, cross her heart and hope to die, secrecy. She will promise to take your words to the grave. That afternoon, she will tell her cross country coach, her boyfriend, her roommate. Word will catch like a venereal disease across campus. You will wake up one morning next week to a text from an ex-lover asking if you are pregnant. You will not answer him, you will, however tell him to go fuck himself. What you really want to tell the boy, your best friend and everyone else, is to keep your baby's name out from between their dirty teeth. But instead, you learn quiet, you learn head down shuffle. You try to make it in and out of the house for the rest of college without speaking to anybody. This will work well for everything but the lonely that waits for you at home like a patient carnivore.

But tonight, you believe your friend. Tonight you are still young. Tonight this is something only you and her know. She gushes about how excited she is to be an "auntie." You glow at how close this sounds to family. She promises to buy your child a baja sweatshirt. You want this to pan out as optimistic as she makes it sound.

You look up the hours for Planned Parenthood because you don't completely trust the generic brand test clenched in your fist. You put the stick in a plastic baggie, will bring it with you tomorrow in case they need proof. You will forget that you have it in your purse. Your hand will brush against it three months from now during physics class and you will burst into tears in front of strangers. The other students in the lecture hall will stare at you. You are used to this by now. No one will ask you what is wrong. You no longer expect or want them to.

But today, you hole up in your room for the night. You don't have the energy to explain this situation to anyone else yet, you barely have the words right now to explain it to yourself. You eat a *Terry's* chocolate orange for dinner, candy left over from your stocking. It tastes like Christmas, like hope delivered in swaddling clothes. You think about how next Christmas might be your baby's first. You watch *Mad Men,* a drama filled with glossy housewives in kid gloves and red lipstick, no older than you. You scroll through Pinterest, collecting pictures of other people's children, onesies with sarcastic phrases stamped across the front, storybook painted nurseries, names for the stranger squatting on your land, under your skin.

You research stay-at-home writing jobs. You create an Etsy account to sell your artwork. You consider selling your soul over the world wide web. You realize too quickly that it will not amount to enough. You go to bed early, only to stare sleepless at the ceiling. You trace the letters "I LOVE YOU" into the skin around your navel. You hope it will be enough.

You wake up at 7 am. You chug water, decaf coffee. You type the address for Planned Parenthood into the GPS, even though in the back of your mind, you already know where it is. It's a small box in a strip mall, beside the laundromat you've been going to for years. You've always just looked around it or through it. You never thought it'd ever be relevant. Until now.

The waiting room is scattered with children's toys, although everyone sitting here is childless. It smells like lemon Lysol and second hand smoke. You are given a phone book thick stack of questions by the receptionist, a woman you've seen before at the bar downtown. Her face is acne pocked and a cheetah print tattoo escapes past the sleeve of her scrubs. Rumor has it, she jumped out of a moving vehicle during a fight with her girlfriend once. You do not want to give this type of lunatic your personal information, but you suppose you have no other choice.

You don't know how to answer most of the questions. *Emergency contact,* you don't want anybody to know about this, even if you're dying. *Number of partners:* 14 men, 3 women, a sum that's larger than your homeroom from your senior year of high school. *How would you feel if this test were positive?* Heartbroken. Determined. Scared. Called to a challenge. Small. Violated.

There is a teen aged girl with a bad dye job and a lip piercing in a cheetah print tank top sitting across the room. Her mother, a tired middle aged woman with a receding hairline sits beside her, feeding her answers.

When you've written all you know, you hand the clipboard back to the receptionist. You try to read a book while you wait, biblical fiction about Samuel, a prophet that refused to hear God, even when He was screaming at him. No, you're not really reading anything, you're staring at the same three words. You wish these words were something poetic, something inspirational. You'd even settle for, "And Jesus wept," a sign from the Almighty that He once cared about lost causes enough to fix them, enough to cry for them like He did for Lazarus. But the words you are staring at are, "and then she," which does nothing but remind you of the uncertainty of your future.

Your name is called and you are handed a cup. You can feel your bladder sitting like broken glass in your gut. You shut the bathroom door behind you. The bathroom is too pink, too soft for the reality you are facing. You get stage fright. You can't pee to save your life. You give up on this like you do with most things. You promise to try again later.

You are led to another room, an office. The receptionist brings you five Dixie cups full of water and then five more. You shoot these back like you used to shoot tequila, while you talk to a grey haired woman whose jawline has dissolved into jowls in her old age. You assume that she is the volunteer doctor. You are in a side office, sitting in an uncomfortable yet padded chair. The appearance says *doctor's office,* but the feeling in the pit of your stomach says *interrogation room.* There is nervous sweat springing from your armpits, your foot jingles against the floor anxiously. The woman re-asks you every question that was in your admittance packet. She comes to a screeching, tire skidding, black ice swerving halt at the number of people you've been with. With eyes wide, she asks, "Would you also like to be tested for STDs?"

This is the moment when you realize that this woman is not on your side, does not know your story or understand it and does not wish to. She asks you this as if your body is a stray dog you've dragged into a vet's office. *Do you think we need to check it for rabies?*

You want to leave. You want to look her dead in the eye and straight face lie and tell her that you actually have AIDS. Instead you assure her that you came up clean at your last check up in August through thin pulled lips.

The woman asks if you got pregnant on purpose. You ask yourself if you have ever done anything on purpose. The woman asks about the father. You assure her that your boyfriend has a "real person's job," although you wince now at how childish this sounds. The woman asks you, in all confidentiality, if you are taking hard drugs. She seems surprised when you say no.

The woman tells you that no one can make you keep this baby, that no matter what anybody says, you have the right to get rid of it. She slips you a list of numbers for mercenaries that will finish all your battles for you. You want to ask her, *but what if I do want to keep it? Who will help me win that war?* But you know, just by looking at you, that this woman has already determined that your child would be better off dead than in your arms.

You swallow back everything you know about eugenics. You try to forget about your white trash ancestors hiding out in the woods against the threat of sterilization round-ups. You try to forget about the Indian children ripped away from their families, to be raised by white people in boarding schools, only to return home as adults not belonging anywhere. People like this doctor have never and will never look at you and see mother. You want to ask this woman if only the "planned" deserve to live, and if so, you want to ask her how you made it this far. You want to ask her who is making this "plan" and could they rearrange it for you? Because the way it is now is breaking your heart.

Instead, when she says "any questions", you ask her if you can still run. You mean run out of this office, out of this building, out of your relationship, out of this baby sized noose she's weaving for you. The woman assumes that you mean at the gym and says, "yes, I encourage it."

You lock yourself in the too-pink bathroom. You pee in their cup and return to the waiting room. The teenaged girl is gone and you wonder about what her verdict was, what her mother will tell her to answer in response to it. A rack of brochures with cartoon illustrations scream titles at you like *safe sex* and *Is my relationship abusive?* Like all advice you've ever been given, it's too little too late.

The receptionist pulls you aside to tell you in her tobacco burned voice what you already know. She knows your boyfriend and her face is as serious as the grave. She hands you another form to fill out. You are dead pan stoic until you get to the question that asks you how many people are in your family, including your unborn child. You write 2 and try not to cry in front of strangers. You write it in ink. No matter what you choose, this is unerasable and irredeemable proof of your baby's existence on this earth. It's no longer just you against the world. And no matter what impossible choice you make, it never will be again.

Hester Prynne's Guide to "A" Words

Questions to consider

"I'm pregnant and I can't keep it," I say it fast, like someone else's coffee order, like I'm trying to get rid of the words as fast as possible so that they can be somebody else's problem. I'm pacing my apartment kitchen floor, clinging to my cell phone like it's a respirator. I can't breathe.

"I'd agree with that decision," Avery says, calmly. This is not what I was expecting. I was expecting rage, denial, an end to the phone call. Avery's temper is a land mine, I walk on eggshells with what I wear, what I say, every day with him. But now he does not abandon me. His voice stays placid, unfaltering, and I am proud of him. "How do you know? Like did you take a test? Are you sure?"

I don't know how to put into words my nerve wracked morning at Planned Parenthood. I don't know how to sum up nearly two hours while a crater faced nurse waited outside the bathroom door for me to overcome my stage fright and pee in a cup. I don't know how to explain the grim, gray-haired physician who had tried to lecture me on what exactly went wrong in my birth control plan. I didn't need her theories, I already knew. Like the song goes— *blame it on the alcohol*—of that Avery and I never had a shortage. I could count on one hand how many sober days we'd had in our relationship. I could not count a day I'd spent with Avery that did not involve sex. I could not count how many birth control pills I'd popped, or apparently how many periods I'd missed.

So I just nod into the phone, without realizing that Avery can't hear me.

***

How will this affect my everyday life?

"Make a pros and cons list," my mother told me over the phone, because despite what I had told Avery, I was not completely sure of my decision. My mother had hardly been surprised when I called her at home, six hours away, and told her. She had been warning me not to get pregnant since I was fifteen, it seemed, while year by year, my cousins dropped with child around me like casualties in some strange war. "I want you to be more than that," she'd always told me. But I wasn't. I wasn't the kid that got out. I was just the kid that no longer lived with them. I wasn't destined for greatness like my parents had always expected of me, I was just trying to get by like everybody else.

"How far along are you?" That's all she asked.

"Twelve weeks," I'd said, and I'd heard her sucking air through her teeth, like trouble was a poison she could siphon outta me.

"Well, that complicates things."

I hadn't stopped crying since the morning at Planned Parenthood, it seemed. The Buddha belly I had blamed on vodka or jalapeno potato chips now bubbled out affectionately. I would not allow myself to imagine what was swimming in there, if it had its father's blue jay eyes or my heart shaped face, its Daddy's freckles or my perma-tan skin. It was a list for now, scrawled in the center of one of my thought journals, where I had penned the original drafts for published essays once. This wasn't a story, this wasn't something I could close my notebook and forget about. Everything I had ever done suddenly seemed so permanent, every choice I'd ever made leading up to this moment seemed like a scar tattooed into my skin. I broke my baby down into bullet points. That's all I could let it be.

Pros:

- You get a baby! (you won't have to kill it)
- This might be your only chance
- If you give it up, you'll always wonder what could have been
- You don't have to do student teaching!
- You will never be lonely again
- Cute baby clothes
- Tax deductions
- abortion= eternal damnation

Cons:

- You are not financially stable. No diploma= no future.
- You can't afford daytime child care
- Avery will either leave you or you will stay together living in misery
- This baby is probably going to have fetal alcohol syndrome
- Your reckless days are over
- You will have a harder time finding someone to love you in the future
- You will get fat
- You will never be a real writer

I count up the pros, I tally up the cons. Even split. I let my hand drop to my stomach, waiting for a kick that my baby is too small to deliver. I need a sign. I need a miracle. I need a million dollars. I need an intercession from God.

***

What are my religious/moral beliefs?

The pews are packed and the sermon has started when I snake my way into St. Joseph's Catholic Church. I've been in exile from my family's faith for the majority of college, choosing to spend Sunday morning on my knees doing an entirely different sort of praying somewhere else. There is a carved crucifix above the altar. Jesus stares down at me from beneath his blood soaked bangs with knowing eyes. His mouth is turned up in a rigor mortis grin. "You disobeyed me," he seems to say. "And now look at what type of shit show you're in."

"Can I sit here?" I ask an old lady with dyed blonde hair.

"Of course sweetheart," she says to me, taken aback by my bloodshot eyes and my shaking hands. I can feel her eyes scanning for track marks when I take off my coat. *Don't trip, lady, not a junkie, just a piece of junk. No worries.*

The priest is preaching the Epiphany, about King Herod killing the babies of Israel in the name of an intelligent career move. He's preaching about the Magi, and how they chose to see a God in something that shit its own pants. I'm praying for an epiphany, praying that I am something more than a Herod in Mary's clothing, but I am struggling to see the difference. I want to be like the Magi, to look up at the sky and know exactly where I am going, to know that someone out there gave a damn enough about me to make a plan for me. But I don't think God thinks about me that much anymore.

"The wise men laid gifts before the infant king, knowing that something so small and humble would someday grow to be greater than them," the priest is droning on behind the pulpit, his glasses slipping down occasionally. "And that is what Alison and Daniel must be hoping for in the future by baptizing their child Natalie here today. Will the parents and godparents please come forward?"

I feel like I am going to throw up. Again, for the fourth time that morning. A woman with waist length brown ringlet hair holds a baby in a white gown. She touches her nose to the baby's, blowing her an eskimo kiss, and it giggles in her face. The baby turns abruptly and stares out at the congregation.

The baby stares at me. Like she knows. She knows what I am about to do in less than a week, to someone who could have one day been her classmate, her best friend, her husband or wife, her coworker, even the guy taking her order at Dunkin Donuts. The baby smiles at me with the same grin Christ gave me when I walked in, as if to laugh at the notion that I could ask God for permission for what I am about to do.

I grab my coat and run down the aisle without putting it on, even though it's about 20 degrees outside. Somewhere in the church, in some other pew another baby starts crying and a young child begs his mother to take him home. Above the door is a bronze statue of the Virgin Mary holding the infant king in her arms. Mary stares down at me coldly. "I faced stoning," she seems to tell me. "I faced death, what is your excuse?"

"Please mother," I whisper as I slam the door behind me. "Just let me come home."

***

Where will you and the baby live?

"Wanna drink?" Avery asks me, waving an Amsterdam bottle at me from where he sits at his desk. My face is tear stained, but nothing has cracked his crooked grin. And nothing would, I guess, it's not like anything's gotten up under his skin. We're in his room, in his house, and I'm wondering why I came. The floor is scattered with empty Twisted Teas and half full Dominoes boxes. A video game is playing on the computer screen while I watch TV. Everything is steeped in weed smoke so deeply that I can no longer smell it. There is an Eminem poster covering the hole Avery punched in the plaster wall last month, when his roommate was blasting music at 2am. The plaster clinging to his knuckles had reminded me of paint smeared across an artist's hand, it seemed natural like that, as if it were a part of his trade. I remember how he'd looked down at his blood speckled fist as if it belonged to someone else. He didn't want to be this way, but it was in his blood. This is not how parents live. This is no place for a child. And I'm starting to think this is no place for me.

"You're joking, right?" I ask him. "I'm not drinking right now. Maybe not ever again."

"Why? We're not keeping it," he says between clenched teeth, his face darkening with the uncertainty he picks up in my voice. His knuckles go white around the neck of the bottle he's holding. "It might as well enjoy its time here, I mean it's gonna be dead soon anyways."

There are tears trailing down my cheeks. I don't have the energy to straight up sob anymore. So I just wipe my eyes. When I go back later to do forensic analysis on where it all went sour, the exact second that I stopped loving him, it will be this moment. Avery is half a fifth of vodka deep on a Monday night and my future dangles by an umbilical cord and he jokes about it like it's something he's seen on TV. Like it's not something I have been raising for nearly three months.

"I mean, it's not alive now, really," he sputters, because he is not an asshole, but because he is young, just 21, like me. He is scared, he is not as smart as I would like him to be all the time. He never had a daddy to teach him how to be one. His father put a bullet in his brain before Avery was born. This is all Avery knows about fatherhood, faded polaroids of a man who left him nothing but his temper and his cold blue eyes. He sits down on the bed next to me, and leans his head against my shoulder, like a puppy apologizing for an accident.

I pull away from him, typing in *Bump and Grind* on my IPod search bar. I'd spent my first week back to class researching pregnancy facts because I couldn't really focus on learning how to teach other people's children when my own child's life hung in the balance. The link pulls up a graphic organizer of a baby's growth from conception to birth. I rub his nose in it.

"Our baby has fingernails and hair follicles," I list. "Our baby has arm joints, she can kick and swallow. Our baby has a face. Our baby has fully functional organs. Our baby is the size of a lime. She has a heartbeat. Don't you dare tell me that she isn't alive."

My baby has all these things, but none of them will be enough to save her because we cannot afford her. She has all my love, but it will not be enough to purchase her life. We scrape through on minimum wage and

Ramen. Avery dropped out of college two years ago, and I can't picture this going anywhere better if I do the same.

Avery places his hand on my stomach as if he's reconsidering for a minute, as if he's actually proud of the lime sized alien swimming beneath my skin.

"This is your daddy," I think to my baby. "And he loves you very much too, he just doesn't know how to do that right."

"Don't get attached to it," Avery says, but I can't tell if he's talking to himself or to me.

I fall asleep later that night with my hand hooked absentmindedly around my stomach. I wake up with my arm at my side and I know that Avery has moved it, frantic with worry that I search for this thing even in my dreams.

"There is no use falling in love with something you can't keep," he tells me. I only wish that someone had given him that advice about me.

***

What choice is best for your mental health?

"I'm keeping it," I tell my mom over the phone. "I really don't have the heart to kill it." I'm driving home from Walmart, a vial of shoplifted prenatal vitamins tucked in my purse in the passenger seat. The words feel good in my mouth, like the inside of a Cadbury egg. They taste like sunshine. And for once in the past week, my chest feels lighter, despite the fact that my tits still feel like bowling balls in my now, ill-fitting bra. I've got the pictures my best friend, Lane, posts of her child on Facebook on a pedestal in my mind. She is broke, sure, but she is always smiling as she scrolls by on my newsfeed. People do this, and they survive. Maybe I can do this too.

"Ok…" my mother says, caught off guard by my change of heart. I don't really feel like explaining Avery's casual reaction, how I couldn't bear to throw a life away with as much certainty as he could. "Then I want you to set up some doctor's appointments. You'll probably be able to know the sex of the baby soon."

"Exciting," I say, trying not to listen to the noise my car's engine is making now that the radio isn't on anymore. It's got one foot in the grave, but I don't have the money to fix it. I don't tell mom that I've already decided the baby is a girl, that her name is Patience. That I've been reading aloud to her the past two nights like she can hear me. If there's still a chance, I want her to be smart, smarter than me. I listen to Disney Soundtracks rather than Eminem around the house now, so that she will grow to be sweet and kind, not bitter and sharpened like me. Not angry and numb like her daddy.

"And get some oversized shirts," she says. "The stuff you wear is too tight, it's not good for the baby."

"Fine, I'll hit up a Goodwill or something," I say, rolling my eyes even though she can't see. She'd been nagging me to loosen up my inseams since I was 16, and now I'd finally have to listen to her. This is the tidy pile of advice my mother gives me: doctors and mumus. I hug the words of wisdom to my chest, praying that her advice is the gateway to her blessing. I catch a glimpse of my face in the rearview mirror, a pair of oversized sunglasses looming over a nicotine tinged smile I haven't seen in at least a week. Bleach burnt hair framing a gradually rounding face. My breasts strain against the confines of their B cup. I can see what they mean about "glowing". I don't think I've ever looked so beautiful. I trace the seat belt pulled tight over my stomach, maybe, just maybe we're gonna be ok.

***

How will this affect the people closest to you?

I'm lying in bed with Pop Tart crumbs and tears pooling on my chest and flecking my tangled yellow hair like strange stars. It's midnight. I haven't spoken to my father directly in years, but he's on the phone now. If I had something to say, Mom usually relayed the message. Nothing was ever good enough for Daddy. I'd hand him a report card of A's and he'd say, this is what he expected. I'd hand him an ink drawing and he'd tell me the eyes didn't quite match. It was enough to drive a person to drink. There was little about my life now that was worthy of telling him about, I already knew about everything I couldn't fix. He knows about the baby now, and I'm too scared to speak.

"I'm not rooting for either side here, Liza. I was that kid," he's telling me. "I was that kid. My mom had me by accident. She wasn't going to stay with my dad, but life makes you desperate, life makes you lonely. She got married because of me, because she felt like there was no other way. She had to live with that choice for the rest of her life. Life is a long time, Liza."

I'm up out of bed and scrambling for a tissue. I'm muffling my crying with the back of my hand because I don't want my dad to know how weak I am. I don't want to keep my roommates up another night with my sobbing echoing through our paper thin walls. When I take my hand away there will be a moon of teeth marks along my knuckles.

"My father used to beat her," My dad continues. "Me and my sister would wake up to see her with a black eye or her face all bloodied from getting it smashed through a window. And that was normal. Your Mamere was a very unhappy woman, Liza, and she had to live with that. There's not a day that goes by that I don't wish she'd made another choice, even if it didn't involve me."

I think about the hole in the wall of Avery's bedroom, the way the sheetrock had caved under his fist. I loved Avery, but could I bank on forever? He had never raised anything but his voice to me, but with a baby bawling in the next room at three am, would I be able to say the same?

"You're strong Liza, you're smart, you're talented," Daddy tells me. "I know that's something I don't tell you enough. But whatever you choose, we will still love you, even if we won't be able to help you."

"I know," I gasp out between sobs, because I can't manage anything else. My worst fear, the end all, seven horsemen of the apocalypse, of all fears has come true. My father knows I'm pregnant, and no one has been shot, no one has been yelled at, no one is disowned. I hang up and stare into the infinity of the ceiling. I think about my childhood home, about how nothing made my father happy, and how my mother blamed herself for this. I think about Lane, about her happy Facebook photos, taken in her parents' house, a happier house than mine had ever been, because she can't afford to move out. And I cannot afford to go home again. Depending on Avery would be repeating history. And I cannot do this alone.

This decision was made for me long before I was born. It was made in each bruise on my Mamere's praline skin, in each time my father raised his voice because that is all he ever learned of fatherhood— loudness and tears. *Always forward, never back*, my father would say, at graduations, at report cards. These were never comments about an individual. It was about the family, his family. My father had succeeded at two things in his life: working his children out of the trailer park and working his body into the ground, his tendons popped and gnarled from masonry like the body of an old tree. He is our family tree. Could I live with myself if I told him it was all for nothing? Could I live with myself if I chose to jump back a generation and follow in my Mamere's footsteps now?

My mother will tell me tomorrow that my father got off the phone that night and threw up. I will wince at the image of this sprawling mountain range man brought to his knees in front of the toilet bowl in my childhood home. She will blame it on his whiskey, I will blame it on the ghosts that always seem to have their teeth sunk into Daddy's shoulders. I will blame it on the fact that this night, he recognized one of his ghosts in me. It is fear, it is remembrance, it is the bitter aftertaste of deja vu, strangling and nauseating.

. He's lived this storyline once already. I cannot make him do it again. *Always forward never back.* And if I have to play God to do it, then so be it. A crucifix never smiled at me anyway.

***

ALIZA DUBE

Do you have a partner who will support you?

"Make me forget what's happening to us," I demand, slamming Avery's bedroom door. He pulls me onto the bed and kisses me like he's trying to swallow me whole. I see him through a collage of tears and the mirage of faces pressed too close together. He's got his hand wedged between the waistline of my now too-tight leggings. I'm peeling his shirt off with my teeth. *American Horror Story: Murder House* is playing in the background. Fake heart-stopping screams echo against the walls. We can hear the splatter of artificial blood, and somewhere beneath the gore the urgent whisper of, *yeah baby, yeah baby, don't stop, don't stop...* but we don't know which one of us is talking anymore.

And when we come to a stop, his eyes closed, nine inches of him still under my skin, he asks me for maybe the fifteenth time this week, "Are you sure you don't want me to go with you?"

And I know that death has filled in the cracks where breathless "I love you's" used to flower up like dandelions through the concrete. The real world has paved us over.

"I'll be fine," I say, even though this is a promise that I've never been able to keep.

***

What choice can you afford?

I have $500 worth of twenty dollar bills wadded up in my sweatshirt pocket. Avery had pressed them into my hand this morning in the driveway and told me to be brave. I am beyond brave; I am numb. I've spent the car ride focusing on where the money came from, not where it is going. Bob Dylan is crooning over the car radio.

You just kinda wasted my precious time, but don't think twice it's alright....

The snow banks outside Planned Parenthood are lined with middle-aged men in flannels and camo hats, stabbing picket signs into the ground. "Take my hand, Not my life," one sign reads. Another has a

166

picture of infant limbs scattered like potpourri. A Green Jesus shakes his head at me from a poster board that probably costs as much as a box of diapers.

I want to scream out the window, *give me the money, and I'll raise it.* Nobody wants me to keep this baby more than me. But I make $300 a month. A baby costs $12,500 a year. I can't break even. Give me the money and I'll save her life. I'll leave Avery, I'll do this on my own. But you can't. You have nothing to offer me, with your hands and your dicks in your pockets trying to ward off the cold.

I stick my middle finger to the car window. But no one bothers to look inside.

Someone on the other end of a speaker buzzes my car in like I'm entering the gates of Oz. The gate shuts behind me. I don't look back. I don't have that luxury.

I can't bring my phone in. I can't bring my purse in. All I can bring in is the money I hand to the overweight receptionist in her glass box and my inhaler, in case I stop breathing. I wish I would stop breathing. The receptionist hands me a clipboard of forms to fill out and a handout that apparently is mine to keep. The handout is printed on purple paper and starts with, "We are women, we are wise, we know when it is right to bring life into the world." I crumple it up and toss it on the floor. I know only that I know nothing but what I cannot afford. There is no wisdom in a dollar sign.

"Liza?" A lady who looks too much like Kathy Bates for me to be comfortable shakes my hand and asks for my birthday. She pulls me into a side room and puts my information into her computer. She hands me more forms to fill out. One confirms that this is my choice and my choice alone. I don't know how to tell her that choices don't happen in a vacuum.

"Ok, so this other form lists off the risks and asks you to initial beside each one," she says and then begins listing off the complications like she's ordering Chinese take out. "Hemorrhaging, incomplete abortion, perforation, infertility, and death." I initial beside each horror, knowing that any one of these risks is preferable to doing nothing at all.

***

What choices are you mentally prepared to make?

The waiting room is filled with *People* magazines and coloring pages, the complex kind for adults because only adults travel here. The room reeks of nicotine, I'm assuming from the large tattooed man with the burn holes in his sweatshirt. His combat boot taps incessantly against the ground. *He really loves her, whoever he's waiting for,* I think to myself. There's a lump in the back of my throat. I want Avery here, I want somebody here, shaking with anxiety over me. But Avery isn't mature enough for this, he can't handle being here. Or maybe I can't handle having him here.

There is a tin can of colored pencils, but all the colorful ones are dulled. Only the shades of brown stick out, proud as skyscrapers. I flip a coloring page over and start writing. I have only a little while for goodbyes. I only have a little while longer to talk to her. I have so much I want to tell her.

Dear Baby,

In a world where I could keep you, you would have eyes as blue as the sky reflected in the ocean, as blue as the wings of jays dancing in the snow, not like mine but like your daddy's. I would read you so many books from the day you were born. I would never stop talking to you, because I have been waiting to tell you everything. I have been stashing away stories for you all my life. I'd sleep with you curled up on my chest because I could never bear to be apart from you for as long as eight hours. I would carry you in a sling across my front so that I could feel your heartbeat against mine. I would kill for you, I would live for you, but I can't seem to do any of that right. I love you, but love alone is never enough.

Mommy loves you very much, but it's not fair to you to ask you to be born when I have nothing to give you. Mommy wants to, but she just can't take care of you right now. So Mommy is sending you to live with your great grandma in heaven for a little while. She will love you and take care of you and when we're both ready, you can come back and find me again. I love you more than you will ever know, even though it might not seem like it right now. I know this is the best choice for the both of us. Until I see you again,
    All my love
    Your Mommy.

***

How will your choice impact your life?

"Liza?" A nurse with a nose ring like mine steps through the swinging doors. She also shakes my hand and asks for my birthday. I can still feel the grit of the anti-anxiety medication they had me take under my tongue and my words come out like cotton.

She leads me to a room with an OBGYN table that reminds me of alien experiments. The foot pads are covered in rainbow cheetah print slip covers. There's a patch of artificial sky on the ceiling. There's a radio playing in the background. Janis Joplin is singing about freedom meaning nothing but nothing left to lose.

"Ok, so I'm gonna leave the room for a minute. Take off your pants, and you can cover up with this pink paper and go ahead and sit on the table," she tells me, breaking everything into bite sized pieces like she is talking to a small child.

I fold my yoga pants, like it matters. I sit on the table and stare at the ultrasound machine, a wand as long as my forearm, that's apparently about to invade my personal space.

The woman with the nose ring comes back in the room with a doctor with a bad perm. The doctor looks like Angela Davis, but white. They smile at me a little too wide, they talk to me a little too soft. They tell me to lay down on the table and I do. They tell me to put my feet on the pedals and spread my knees as far apart as I can, and I do. There are forceps lodged like jaws between my legs. I stare up at the square of fake sky and wish I was anywhere else but here.

The doctor breaks the procedure into bite sized pieces.

"Ok, so we're gonna take an ultrasound now, to see what we're dealing with," She says.

The ultrasound is silent. I watch the doctor's face look at my baby, a baby I will never give birth to, an infant I will never get to hold in my arms. A face I will never see.

"Do you want to know anything about this ultrasound?" she asks me.

"No," I say, even though I will spend every day after this regretting that word, regretting that I never even took the time to look at her before I put her in the ground.

"Wait," I say, because there is one thing I have to know. "Is it a boy or a girl?"

The doctor winces at this question. It is easier to not ask questions about the condemned. There is no point collecting data on what will never be.

"The fetus is female," she says clinically, before going on to explain the rest of the procedure. I can barely hear her. Instead my brain is screaming *Patience* like it's the only English it has left. But it's already too late. It's always been too late.

The doctor explains as she goes, but I have stopped listening. She disinfects what she needs to. She applies local anesthesia. She opens up my cervix, and replaces it with what seems like lava in my gut.

"You can hold my hand if you need to," the lady with the nose ring tells me.

"No," I say and squeeze her fingers for dear life.

I can feel the outline of my uterus beneath my skin, like it's trying to claw its way out of my abdomen.

"You're doing fine, you're a rockstar," nose ring tells me. I don't feel like a rockstar.

I'm thinking of the early months, when Avery and I were happy, watching *Shameless* in his room, half stoned and half asleep. On the TV, an old Native American man walks into a house trailing a herd of children behind him.

"Why does he have so many kids?" Avery had asked me.

"Indians always have a lot of kids," I tell him, although I can only speak for my cousins and not necessarily an entire race. Avery hugs me tight and kisses the back of my neck.

"Then where are your kids, Liza?" He asked jokingly.

Where are your kids, Liza? The question echoes in my head now, blocking out the whir of the vacuum. *Where are they?*

My baby leaves in a jar covered with a paper lunch bag, like something a wino would drink out of underneath the interstate. The doctor is leaving to count the pieces, to make sure there's nothing left in me. I don't need her body count. I can already tell her there is nothing left.

***

What choices are impossible for you?

My mother tells me God forgives. My boyfriend tells me we dodged a bullet. My father tells me I have a bright future.

I wake up sometimes with my hand hooked over my flat stomach, where my hip bones are starting to resurface, like fossils rising from the mud. I throw my feet over the side of the bed. Then I remember and it feels like a bullet to the back of my skull. I run a comb through the hair I've shorn short in mourning. It sticks up in unruly directions like the feathers of a dead bird on the highway. I drink my coffee. I go to class. I live life in bite sized pieces. And I try not to choke.

How to Fall in Love

Your baby dies unborn. Unloved. Fatherless. It's ok, because its mother never really wanted it anyways. "We'll get through this together," your boyfriend tells you. You're not even sure if it was his to begin with. It doesn't matter. It's been two weeks since you've seen him. It's Valentine's Day. You're alone.

You tell yourself you're going to have a glass of wine. You watch Disney movies with the cat. You look up to find the bottle empty. Your bedroom has recently started to look more crypt than boudoir. You stumble to the kitchen for blueberry vodka. You text a stranger. No, not a stranger, your friend's roommate. The two of you make a pact. I won't tell if you won't. "Are you home alone?" he asks you.

You type back "yes" with a winky face that is more flippant than you feel. Yes, yes, you are always alone.

You spill sriracha on your bedroom carpet till it soaks in like a blood stain. You don't try to clean up your mess. The damage is already done.

You take a shower to stay awake. It's one a.m. and you're still waiting for something, anything to happen. You think about baptism. You wonder aloud if you can drown while standing up. You wipe the soap out of your eyes. You think about your mother combing your damp hair before bed. You think of her rubbing your closed eyes with her fingertips and promising only good dreams as if it were a magic spell. You've always had terrible nightmares. You don't anymore.

You pop a zyquil so that you can pass out without dreaming. Without thinking, when this is all over.

You let your friend's roommate in the front door. You realize you actually have nothing to say to this person, that you've never had a conversation. You have nothing to talk about anyway. What's there to say? What's up, Liza? Ya know, just this, what we're up to here, but with different people, in different beds. Your life is nothing but a collection of stories that nobody wants to hear. You ask if he wants to watch Netflix. The two of you agree on *That 70's Show*.

The boy has a gap between his two front teeth. You mentally debate whether you find this appealing or not while your tongue plays behind the back of them. You let him in your shirt, in your pants, up under your skin. You let him pull your hair back like he's trying to scalp you.

You demand that he wear a condom because you've had a scare and you're not going back there again.

"What kind of scare?" he'll ask. You're hoping he hasn't noticed the goodie bag from Planned Parenthood that's sitting on your dresser. The bag with the brochure, with the helpline. Call if you have any questions. Call if you are upset. You are angry about everything. You question everything. You call no one.

"I don't really wanna talk about it," you tell him. And you don't.

A crucifix hangs like a convict in the hollow of your cleavage. It smacks the boy straight in the forehead while you fuck, but he doesn't seem to mind. You've always worn irony on a chain around your neck, you hadn't remembered to take it off for the night.

You'll finish watching the episode, your naked thighs draped over his lap. You'll let him go home after that. You don't really want him there anyways. He won't come over again.

You dream that your baby lived. That she got adopted. That she is sixteen and you meet her on a train, but neither of you can recognize the other. That you pass each other like strangers.

Your boyfriend will wake you up in the morning with a "Good

Morning Beautiful" text. You don't feel beautiful.

You drive to his house with the intention of breaking up with him. He'll clasp a silver necklace around your throat that reads, "I love you to the moon and back." A belated Valentine's Day present. You say that you love him too. You tell yourself never again. You tell yourself this is where you belong. You fuck through a *Hangover* movie marathon. You both joke about how your father will make fun of your boyfriend for being a video game nerd at your wedding. Your boyfriend will press an iced cold Twisted Tea can to your bare breast just to hear you scream.

You try to fall asleep, each of you facing different walls. You wait for him to start snoring. You go outside and smoke a Marlboro Red in a snowbank. You look up at a smile of a moon in a crisp mean winter sky. You wonder about how far the moon is from where you're standing. You ask yourself if it's possible to love someone that much, let alone double that. You tell yourself that you are exactly where you are supposed to be. That everything happens for a reason. That any of it means anything at all.

You hear the door open behind you. You let your boyfriend wrap a blanket around your shaking shoulders. You let him lead you back to bed. You pop a Zyquil.

You dream that your baby is sitting on the moon like the child from the Dreamworks logo. She's crying, she needs you. You run until you can feel muscles snapping in your legs like overworked fishing lines. You stretch your arms out as far as they will go until you can hear joints popping loose from their sockets. You jump as high as you can until your heels ache from the impact of your soles hitting the frozen ground again and again like pistons going nowhere. No matter what you do, no matter how you tear yourself apart, you can't reach her. You wonder how it's possible to love something this much.

Daisy Buchanan's Guide to
Extramarital Affairs

The jukebox is playing some overcooked country song about first loves. Everyone in this bar looks too jaded to believe in what this southern boy is preaching in his lyrics. In a bar full of threadbare and cheap beer cynics, I am their queen, posted on a barstool in a Hooters tank top and booty shorts. I'm checking out other guys over my boyfriend's shoulder. There is a hickey I am not even trying to conceal at the edge of my neckline, from a booty call at the break of dawn this morning.

It hadn't been love, not even like. The boy that morning had been an empty and big headed soccer goalie who made fun of me for my taste in mumble rappers and little else. The goalie had a bad habit of ruining my sheets, and an even worse one for leaving money on my nightstand to pay for their launder. The stack of quarters had glinted at me, cold and blasphemous as Judas's silver. I had always thought that I was worth more than $3.25, but I guess, as with everything else, I had been wrong. The past year has taught me ruthless, has taught me savage, has taught me all the reasons I need to drink. Has taught me why I need and belong to bars like this one, even if I do not belong to the people I am here with.

Avery is not the first to love this body of mine, just the first that ever wanted to do something more than rent it, when it could not even lay claim to its own self. Now I look at his *Mad* comics kid face, worn and faded in the neon light across the table from me. I think of how rarely I see his riot toothed smile anymore. He is beginning to realize that I am a fixer upper. A money pit. I am not worth what he paid for me. This is a lesson he is learning each day, learning right now when his sister asks me how many men I've been with but him, and I cough up sixteen ghosts onto the bar room table without thinking or blinking. I have lost track of how many ways I am breaking his heart.

I have been looped in to another double date from Hell, me and Avery, his sister and her abusive boyfriend that Avery spends his free time plotting to kill. I'd rather be home, re-reading *Gatsby* for the third time. But instead I'm here, stuck in this dead town bar, this valley of ashes between my future and my past. Smoking is not permitted inside, but the whole place reeks of nicotine. My whole life reeks of nicotine. It is May and the college students have traveled to greener pastures for the summer. I have nowhere else to go. I am growing roots here under this bar stool. I am becoming what they call a "regular" and the thick armed bouncer at the door no longer checks my ID. I do not wish to belong to this place. I had once wanted my resting place to be something greater than the wall of amber glinting bottles behind the bar and the looped neon of Bud Lite signs. I try not to notice how Sister's red veined eyes stretch wider than her anime pupils when I say my numbers.

Avery's sister is an old lady at thirty. Her hair falls down to her waist some kind of dead mouse color, riddled with dollar store hairspray. She proclaims herself beauty queen, I think bog witch. She's got frown lines, nicotine wrinkles aging around a tired mouth. The skin under her eyes is getting weary of holding up her sockets; they've seen so much and yet nothing at all. She is the ghost of what will become of me if I stay here. And I shiver in the early June barroom heat.

"And you, what's your total?" I ask, trying desperately to bury the skeletons in my closet in a comparison contest.

"Seven," she says cautiously, like if she had known what I was going to say than she wouldn't have asked, at least not in front of my boyfriend, her brother. At least not in front of her boyfriend, a baseball cap wearing skid who leaves skid marks on pavement until his tires run bald, regardless of the fact that nobody has money to replace them. A man who leaves skid marks on Sister's back, purple, green and blooming behind the glass of the shower door. He hammers his name up her vertebrae with his fists like she is something to remodel.

In nature, rats often get their tails tangled. When this occurs, the rat either has to amputate or live out the rest of its life alongside whoever is on the other side of the knot. These snarls can include up to 32 rats. My tale has become ensnared in that of those around this sorry bar island table. I'm plotting my escape though, bracing myself for when I will have to cut off a piece of my own person to set myself free. I'm not ready yet, but every step I take, every word I speak here feels more and more like a trap.

When Sister speaks of scandalous women that they grew up with, girls who give blow jobs and venereal diseases before they are even given their high school diplomas, Skid always chimes in that that particular individual is a "dirty girl," with a tone that contains more hope than disgust. It creeps me out. Now, after hearing my tally, I have this sick feeling in the pit of my stomach that I now fit this category for him, that I have joined this club that I didn't even know existed.

My boyfriend doesn't acknowledge that he has heard anything I've said. We have a "don't ask, don't tell" policy when it comes to my past. Even when it comes to my present. It's easier if he can make me up and play pretend in the few hours I'm with him than to try to swallow the truth; that the tally has risen since I met him, that it is partially his fault for leaving me alone so many cold winter weekend nights when starless skies screamed lonely. He has given me too many reasons to stray.

He never asks about the bruises, mouth sized like moths looking for the light against the waistline of my hips. Never asks about the outlines of ghost fingers lined like prison bars or stanzas against the misplaced ivory of my windpipe. He does, however, comment on how good I've gotten at blowjobs, asking me between stolen breaths if I had been "taking classes." I don't answer, I never do. I never really talk much anymore anyway. I've run out of things to say. We survive by talking around what hurts. Around Sister's bruises and mine, as if their blue were puddles and the boys were always scared of getting their feet wet.

Skid goes to mock knock over a glass of water, I glare at him against the dim lit table and screech, "I'm wearing white!" a proclamation of a purity and a modesty that I apparently do not deserve, have not earned.

"Yeah, a Hooters tank top," Sister scoffs. "And it's probably well worn in too."

I now have a small understanding for why Skid feels the need to hit her so often. Avery's face goes up in red like wildfire. Who is she to hold her seven heaven high above my sweet sixteen? I want to say, well at least none of mine ever beat me...but I bite my tongue. The feminist in me recoils at all the ugly that has grown in me. I scour her face for what she expects to see in mine: shame, embarrassment, remorse? I am indifference. I am irreverence. I am sweet apathy. I am nothing more than a product of the men who have raised me.

"Yeah, it's pretty broken in," I grin at her, chin high and defiant. Avery was not the first or even the most recent. He will not be the last. No one is allowed to own this body but me.

***

In the early days, when they were still in love, Scott liked to write love letters to Zelda about princesses locked away in towers, far up above the grimy reach of any man but her prince. Zelda told him to stop this, she did not like the idea of being put in anyone's box, not even his.

Zelda was the madcap of her hometown, Montgomery, Alabama. Her father prevailed over the local court and she made her own laws up as she went along. She danced on tables at the local country club. She ran barefoot through the streets despite her mother's warnings that this would be the ruin of her. She swam in a nude colored leotard, always as close to naked as she could manage. She once kissed a man with a moustache simply because she had wanted to know what it felt like.

Zelda was close to suffocating in Montgomery. She could already see what life would be if she stayed there. A proper marriage to one of the ridiculous boys that swore often and loudly that they would die for her. A house, with a porch swing, sweet tea clinking with ice and melting, lazy afternoons. A couple children or three. She would wake one day to find herself an eccentric old woman, a local legend faded into dust and cobwebs. An arthritic shadow of her former self corseted into a shape that her neighbors were able to recognize. She could hear them now: "thank goodness Zelda has finally settled down, just look how much happier she is now that she's quit it with all her gallivanting."

But Zelda, in her heart, knew that she would never be content with ordinary happiness. Zelda knew she was destined for something, she wasn't exactly sure what, but *something*. When she had danced with Scott that first night at the country club she could almost taste it. Scott was like no one she had ever met. He crooned in her ear about the books he would write, the places he would travel. *And didn't she know that a distant uncle of his had written the star spangled banner?* His words were gonna take him places and all he was wondering was if he could take her with him.

Zelda considered the offer for a while after they kissed goodbye on the judge's porch swing. She considered it while she wrote him letters, asking him to prove his worth to her. *Bring me a book, a royalty and you will have my hand,* she bargained. Zelda thought about it as she kissed nothing boys on sticky Alabama summer nights, with her eyes slammed shut. If she wasn't looking, she could still pretend she was kissing Scott instead. Historians are unsure if she loved Scott for Scott's sake, or if she loved the way he looked everything like an escape route, a train ticket to another world. Zelda knew, that if she could just hang on to Scott's coat tails long enough, maybe she'd have the chance to become that *something* she'd always been looking to be. Maybe she would be able to know what that something was before she died.

***

Me and Avery are sitting on Sister's bed. Sister and Skid are under the covers, a timeworn patchwork quilt that some ancestor must have stitched with love, but this art was lost long ago. We don't know how to make anything but problems. I'm wearing a black lace skirt and the way I am sitting, I know Skid can see the whole world. There's no way I can adjust this without drawing further attention, so I pretend it isn't happening while he doesn't even pretend not to look.

The Godfather is playing on the screen in the background, because I guess that's what you do when your life has gone off the rails, you watch some other poor bastards on TV and say well at least my life ain't like that, at least I'm better off than those poor fuckers.

Sister and Skid are living here, at Avery's grandmother's house in this room next to Avery's. Avery lost his job, because who knew you couldn't do lines at your desk and then still expect to get paid? Avery lost the trap house. It's just as well, I recognize every ghost that Avery ever claimed to have seen in those beer spattered halls. The shadow of a young girl he had seen tumbling down the stained carpet stairs, the child's laughter he had heard from the bathroom when no one else was home. They had all been my baby girl calling out to us from the future. Telling us to get ready, to be ready. We didn't listen. But maybe that is what happens when children are made in the shadow of a graveyard, the dead inevitably come to take back what has always been theirs.

This room is scattered with ashtrays, litter boxes and garbage bags bulging with clothes. It's so crowded that I honestly can't tell how many cats are in here at any given time. There's a tiger striped one on the bed now, tailless, half bobcat, half tabby, and I'm scratching behind his ears for dear life because I never know what to do with my eyes or my hands in social situations. Avery pushes me into scenarios all the time for which I have no script.

Skid, Sister and Avery are all smoking cigarettes, even though no one on this bed has money for their own place of residence or even money for food. There is always money for tobacco, cash for booze. Avery's grandmother comments on this often. She is an old woman with bifocal glasses and a 1950's rolled up your shirtsleeves attitude. Everything she ever got, she worked for, her husband worked for. We, on the other hand, have worked hard to lose everything we've been given.

This is not how Avery's grandmother imagined her retirement, her husband dead, her grandchildren grown and dependent, stinking up her house and staining her ceilings. A house she will lose before the year is up.

"Why couldn't I have just died before all this?" she asks us often, and she is dying, a tumor sitting like a pearl in her lungs, but not quick enough according to her. And I marvel at how life can get so bad that you'd rather die than try to figure out where your next round of groceries is coming from.

On the TV, there is a woman, not a very pretty one, but a very Italian one, with Arabica eyes and a regal nose. She is the type of woman that will probably inflate after she pops out a few kids, you can see the inevitability in the roundness of her hips, in the ambiguity of her cheek bones. But for now she is radiant in an Italian field and a boy is looking at her as if she were the Holy Ghost. His friends are warning him that a woman is the most dangerous thing in the world, but he can't take his eyes off the buttons that go all the way up her back. I list off the things that are more dangerous than women silently to myself: *poverty, ignorance, guns, drugs, pitbulls, oncoming traffic, bad health insurance, Donald fucking Trump....*

Avery is babbling on about his friend, Tyler's, baby, "He's so cute! And his feet are so big!" I am trying not to listen. Our baby is dead, her feet shredded like potpourri in a hazardous waste bin somewhere. She doesn't even have a grave. Avery has no business praising another child when he took mine away from me. He has no right to exclaim over how responsible a dad Tyler has become when he himself refused to grow up, man up for me. I am tired of carrying the dead weight of my child around with me. I have no choice though; you can't leave the idea of a baby at the fire station, no orphanage will shelter murdered promise. So I hoist the memory of Patience a little higher on my hip in my mind and try to carry on until the next time someone mentions an infant and the burden of her bones digs in a little farther. Sister is eyeing me like I'm a landmine, wondering which one of Avery's words is going to set me off. He is too stupid to notice that he is taking an evening stroll through a battlefield.

I turn my attention back to the screen over Avery's shoulder. The staring boy from the field is clasping a necklace around the dangerous girl's swan neck. The stone on the necklace gleams green, an unreachable light so far away from where I'm sitting. She is exclaiming "yes" like they are having sex on screen, but they aren't. The staring boy is just simply asking her to marry him. He wants her to have his babies, to be his wife, to live happily ever after with him for the rest of their lives. I've never seen the end of this movie, but I hope the staring boy gets murdered, and I hope the dangerous girl gets fat.

I tune back into Avery's conversation long enough to hear him say, "I think the best relationship I ever had was with Hayley." I turn away as if I'd been slapped. Sister shoots Avery a *What the fuck is wrong with you?* look. I pretend I didn't hear. I already know that I have never and will never be anybody's favorite anything.

Later, when we shut out the lights for the night, Avery will apologize for this. Later he will say he didn't mean it. Later he will eat me out for 20 minutes, trying to force something like forgiveness from the graveyard of my lips. Instead I will shrug and tell him I don't care. I will wait until he falls asleep, then I will excavate myself out of his arms, lying next to him, but not with him anymore. I will not betray angry, I will not betray heartbreak, I am apathy incarnate, nothing more. I'm too tired to be anything more. There is nothing left for me to care about.

But what I really want to ask him is, do you think you're the best I've ever done, or the best I could ever do? I want to ask him how many girls he called "my" before me. I want to throw up the number of times I've cheated on the bedspread like a tequila hangover and watch him try to clean up the mess I've made of us. I want to drown every apology he's ever given me in the oceans of men I've known. I want to ask him what the point of love is, when the thing that love has made is dead. I want to tell him that he doesn't have to apologize, you can't hurt someone who expects it by now.

***

Scott did prove himself, carved Zelda's letters up like a butcher to write about one side of paradise. Scott had found his muse, his Zelda whispered in his ear at every click of the typewriter. Her chocolate box face and devil may care attitude glancing up from the page got him a publication where no other drafts had before. This girl was his guardian angel, his inspiration, his leading lady. He had to keep her around by any means necessary.

Scott wrote to Zelda to tell her the news. Wrote to send for her. Wrote to tell her that life as she knew it was coming to an end. She was to meet him in New York. They would be wed at Saint Patrick's cathedral upon her arrival. Let's make this perfectly clear, the only two people who were in favor of this union were Scott and Zelda themselves. Zelda even had to pace in the rectory to keep her feet warm, second thoughts were turning her toes to ice. Her family quickly departed and she embarked on the rest of her life, a barrage of orange blossoms, money troubles and a husband, a man she realized now, that she barely knew.

Zelda soon became disillusioned with Scott, the whole adventure of it. She never really changed. She became frustrated with Scott who was constantly angry with her for remaining to be the girl he fell in love with. Everything she said still sounded like flirting, it was an accent that she was never really able to shake. Scott had one affair after the other, getting increasingly more suspicious of Zelda after each of his flings. He saw in Zelda what he could not, did not wish to see in himself. Scott had a habit of victimizing himself. Always thought the world was looking down its nose at him. (It is rumored that he had a notoriously small dick, so what more can we really expect of him). The only thing in his life that he really had control over was Zelda, and he took full advantage of that.

Later in her life, Scott would brag about being able to orchestrate her moods as if she really were a character of his own creation. Zelda was starting to believe that maybe she was. Zelda gave birth to a daughter, a fact that filled her with dread. The world had a habit of swallowing pretty little girls whole. Zelda knew this better than anyone. Zelda eulogized, "Let her be a beautiful little fool, that's the best thing a girl can be in this world." If Zelda had been a fool, she would have stayed in Montgomery, where the world was steady and sober and sure. Not this wavering horizon, not this wild goose chase, arms outstretched, trying to scrape the foundation of some elusive dream that didn't even belong to her in the first place.

Zelda grew bored and angry. She attempted an affair, which fizzled and suffocated under Scott's clenched fist. This indiscretion became a dinner guest anecdote, Zelda's pain paraded as punchline. Zelda was tired of being Scott's character, she was going to write her own story. But it was already too late.

Zelda ran a forensic analysis on what her life had become, tried to locate the fracture, where it had all started to come apart. The country club, her ballet performance, Scott staring admiringly, love at first sight, drunk, up at her from the audience. She would become a dancer.

She started lessons, thirteen hours a day, spinning circles. Always going in circles, like a prey animal looking both ways for an escape route. She tied her legs to the bedposts at night to try to train her feet to turn out as they should and she thought, for a moment, it was nice to actually be as restrained as she felt in all her waking hours. She bought a dance hall looking glass for their house, so that she could practice from home, a whore house mirror, Scott called it. To him everything regarding Zelda had become all slur and bruises. Zelda grew thin and anxious, her tendons pulled as taut as her nerves. She twirled and twirled. Day in and day out. She was getting dizzy, she was bound to fall.

***

In the morning, we are scattered land mine limbs, a leg draped over a back, my fist scrunched up into my forehead because I am always fist fight ready, even in sleep. Avery's hand encompasses one of my knee caps, a place I've never felt needed holding. My elbow is jammed into his spine, but he doesn't seem to mind. Pins and needles creep down the synapses of my still nerves. My teeth taste like someone else's dinosaur breath. Our eyes are closed but our noses are touching. Our bodies don't seem to have gotten the memo that we are learning how to fall out of love, that we shouldn't sleep this way anymore. What will I do with all this muscle memory when he is nothing but a memory to me?

Avery tells me that I am bad luck, that when I sleep on his bed all the remotes crash to the floor, all the sheets peel back from the mattress like cadaver skin, as if compelled by some supernatural force. I want to tell him that I am a broken mirror, I want to scream at him to get as far away from me as humanly possible because all he is doing by staying is getting his fingers cut on all my edges. I want to yell that I do not forgive, not him and not myself, not for the truth we say in the dark and drunken night. For the moments when we forget to walk around and we tromp right through the puddle of what hurts.

He only clasps me in his embrace, his arms close and final as a coffin lid over my ribcage. He tucks the fleeing blankets about my restless shoulders, and I feel as though I am being buried alive. He kisses the knot of vertebrae at the nape of my neck as if it were a lucky penny.

"My life was great until you showed up," he says. It's meant to be a joke. We both know that it really isn't. I want to tell him to go fuck himself for blaming me for all his bad decisions, but I really can't say anything about it, because lately I've been blaming him for mine. Blame, responsibility, fault, it's a game of hot potato we play, throwing them back and forth, trying to save ourselves from getting burned.

A part of me thinks that, maybe, what has gone so far off the rails in Avery's life is that he doesn't have the common sense to run from me, as every other thing that breathes was born knowing. He was never that good with survival instincts, every childhood story he tells me about a concussion or a car accident ends in me asking him, "how are you still alive?"

"Just luck, I suppose," he'll always say.

He's been on a bender for four days, little sleep. His pupils are wide heads up pennies and I shiver away the image of a Victorian corpse with a pair of two pence sealing it's eyes for good luck on its way into the ground.

He has been on unemployment for two weeks. He calls to renew it every Sunday morning in the bathroom while he takes a piss. He calls this responsibility; I call it defeatism. They have lost a house, and are losing another. Our baby is dead, and with the way things are I hate myself for knowing that this is for the best. His new room is only big enough for his mattress and a thin ribbon of hardwood floor. It is no bigger than a mausoleum. I am claustrophobic in this room, in his arms, in this life. I am meant for bigger things than this, I tell myself, but I am not sure that this is true anymore.

I am leaving soon, for three months, to supervise other people's children at a summer camp. I worry that things will only get worse when it is just him and a mattress in his shoe box of a room. Or maybe my absence will be a detox, slowly sucking the poison from his life and mine. I am not naive enough to believe that we will survive this.

I am too jaded now, too bone-ground, life-weary tired to believe that things will get better. We are early morning kissing trying to ward off the hopeless beyond our bedroom door. Our tongues are heavy will apologies we will never say. We do not belong to each other anymore; we have fallen too far from fortunate now to claim that. But here is his mouth and my lips, his hand and my wrist, heart against ribs. We can pretend that no other names exist but ours, at least for awhile longer.

"I love you," he says into the nape of my neck, like a necklace he is clasping there. I don't say it back. Instead I think of what Jordan Baker has to say about the Buchanans in *Gatsby*. *Neither of them can stand the person they're married to.* I think of how that story ends, all bullets and car wrecks and low funeral attendances. I wonder if there's a way for me to back out of this storyline now, quietly, without rustling any pages. Or are the cogs of this life already set in motion, chugging away, straight lined and dead end tracked to a great and then one day? Daisy survives the novel, you remind yourself, even if no one else does. And for this morning, that's enough.

I trace the letters to "I'm sorry" into Avery's shoulder as he drifts back off to sleep. I don't know if he notices. I don't know if I am apologizing for things I have already done or for what I am about to do.

***

The more Scott drank, the crazier Zelda became. The crazier Zelda became, the more Scott drank. A friend once described the couple as a pair of barnacles, clinging only to each other. Sharp and ugly to one another, even though, on their own, they would surely die.

Scott punched Zelda full in the face. Her sister begged her to leave him. Zelda swallowed a mouthful of her own blood and told her not to speak of what she didn't understand. Scott began to flirt with other women in front of Zelda. Zelda threw herself down a flight of stairs. She filled their bathtub with her clothes and lit it on fire. Scott tried to scavenge through the wreckage that had become Zelda, tried to find some dental record of what he had once loved in this chocolate box faced girl. His creation, the character he had written, was not going as planned. It was time to scrap the draft.

Scott placed Zelda in institution after institution. *Schizophrenia,* some doctors said, although they could never fully prove a diagnosis. What was really so crazy about a woman learning to live on eggshells? What else could really be expected of a woman who was expected to live with a fist poised at her face? What else could be expected of a mother so often deprived of her child?

The manic pixie dream girl, as we have come to know her, never makes it to the end of the story. She disappears somewhere in the plot. Nobody ever asks where she goes when she goes. Maybe it's because we don't want to know. Maybe it's because in our hearts we know that she might be sitting next to Zelda, in electroshock therapy, being punished for all the parts of her that made us want her in the story to begin with. When women have outgrown their use as plot device, where do they go?

Zelda wanted her narrative back. She wrote her own novel, loosely autobiographical. Scott became enraged. Her life was his writing material, her stories, *she*, belonged to him. He poured over the manuscript, ravenous as a vulture, plucking out whatever of her words he wanted and leaving her the bare bones with which to attach her byline.

Scott died before Zelda, of a heart attack, proving against all odds, that he did possess this organ in the first place. Reportedly, Death came for him while he was having sex with another woman, but Zelda was beyond caring. Upon his death, her eczema cleared up, her skin no longer felt as though it were on fire. She could breathe for the first time in years. She did not attend his funeral, the first time she would visit his grave site would be in a casket.

Zelda would die in a mental hospital, still high up in the tower Scott had cloistered her in

so long ago. A kitchen fire spread up to her top floor room, where she had been locked in for the night. She died unheard, she died painful. She died in a box. She died surrounded by her paintings that she had spent her stay creating; tortured fairy tale scenes of scattered limbs and stoic royalty. Paintings of Biblical moments, of Bethlehem, a holy family bathed in Godly light. The girl who had spent the majority of her life raising Hell now seemed to be consumed by it on her deathbed. She couldn't help but look forward to telling Scott she told him so; that princesses were no safer kept in towers after all.

How to Go Crazy

It is your 22nd birthday. You wake up on your boyfriend's sheet stripped mattress. You blink at the cigarette stained ceiling, you roll over, shove him in the shoulder. "Wake up, it's my birthday!" you say. His blue jay eyes will shoot you a panicked look. He has forgotten it entirely. You had made him a card for his birthday, in the first and blissful days of your union, cartoon representations of you and him kissing hand drawn across the front. You had wrapped a Twisted Tea can in Disney Princess wrapping paper because that's all you had. When you apologized for this he looked at you gravely and said, "It's alright, I am a Princess." You had laughed, careless and too loud. You do not laugh so much anymore.

Your boyfriend gets you nothing but an excuse and an apology. You get yourself a new tattoo. You tell yourself that this is enough.

That night you lay on your stomach on his bed with a Pepsi bottle full of Jack Daniel's. You are trying to forget what day it is. On the TV, a blonde in a man's button up dress shirt wanders around a spacious and clinically clean apartment. "I need to get rich someday, so that you can wear one of my dress shirts and wander around the house in it," your boyfriend tells you. You kiss him because this is the kindest way to tell him that this is impossible.

Your boyfriend traces the red rimmed silhouette of your fresh ink with a nicotine stained finger. The design is an Alice in Wonderland for those who never ask, like Avery. For you the design is your lost girl, Patience, posted as an angel on your shoulder. It is proof that she is always with you, no hiding, no denying.

"It suits you," your boyfriend says to you. You smile, looking over your shoulder at him. You spend your birthday night getting obscenely drunk in his bed, watching Disney movies. This day marks a brief renaissance for your love affair. Some would look on it as resurrection, but all you can see between the sheets are death throes. Your hair has grown back some, your skin darkening just enough in the May sun. You no longer look like girl interrupted and for that you suppose he is grateful, for that he has come again to worship at your alter.

The winter has taught you that no one was coming for you. No matter how many bones you barred, how many seams in yourself you ripped open, no one was coming for you. You spent the spring learning stucco and plaster. You looked in the mirror now and saw a restored porcelain doll, there are hairline cracks beneath the surface, but it's ok, no one bothers to look that deep anyway.

"How so?" you ask him. He is not a smart man, but sometimes he has childlike revelations that you find almost poetic in their twisted innocence. He is writing material, even if he would never be boyfriend material, never be husband material, even though he had proven not to be father material.

"Because everyone thinks you're crazy," he says. "but you're actually really cool. Like Alice."

You smart at the comment. You had spent most of your life trying to outrun crazy. You put up wallpaper, drew up curtains trying to keep it from peeking through. But the walls were peeling now, the wind was blowing too hard now. Love is meant to be someone who goes insane with you. These nicotine tinged fingers on your shoulder would never be that.

You used to think that smoking was attractive when Adam did it. His lips had tasted like martyrdom, like rebellion, handheld fireworks and sparks. Adam is two seasons gone. Avery is nothing but a generic knock off of all that you had once loved. On Avery's tongue, Marlboros taste like rotting. Like the blood on both your hands. Like hanging your head out the car window morning, dog sick tired while a bummed cigarette spit cusses at you from between his fingers. There isn't anything poetic anymore for you in slow death, in chosen death.

"People think I'm crazy?" you ask him, it's a dirty word on your tongue, blackened and brittle between your teeth as something hauled up from a house fire. "Why do they think that?"

He doesn't cite any of the evidence he could have, but a thousand moments flit through his blue jay eyes. When you refused to drink while pregnant, even though you weren't keeping it. And when he asked you why you answered, "Respect for the dead."

When he came home from work one day to find you wandering the graveyard neighboring his house, like a child exploring a zoo. You had looked at him bright eyed and said that the oldest stone went back to 1795.

When you would send him text messages out of the drunken blue, written only in French. He would ask you the next day, "What does this mean?" You would say, "it's a list of all the ways I love you." Really, it was always an obscene rant of all the ways he had ever made you feel more girl than woman, more woman than human. It was never something you were willing to explain in any language he understood.

When you sat on his lap in a stranger's basement and had woven threesome stories for him like it was a recitation of *the Night Before Christmas*. He never knew what to do with your coughed up histories, he always assumed you were lying, sadly this was never the case.

"Whatever, I guess it's a compliment," you shrug. You have a bad habit of flipping and refurbishing any insult thrown your way: *slut, bitch,* now *crazy*. You don't find anything poetic anymore in this type of optimistic death, in this death you did not choose.

You know that by the time you next put needle to skin Avery will be long gone. He will never get the chance to call you crazy again, or anything else for that matter.

A Self-Made Girl's Guide to DIY Tattooing

Step 1: You should not choose an area that is near open sores, boils, abrasions or infected wounds

***

"Text me everyday," Avery begs of me, his voice sounding wounded, standing ankle deep in the dirt of his driveway. We are in a drought. I can see it in the dust between my toes, can feel it in the crack of my lips. He had not remembered that I was leaving for camp today. Would not have remembered at all if I had not texted him last night about it. I thought of how much more preferable that would have been, to slip out of his life for three months like a thief. But some part of me needed to know that somebody would miss me. Even if it was only the Mountain Dew mouth man in front of me.

"I can't make any promises!" I say, it's the same thing I tell my mother when she tells me to "behave myself" as if I wasn't already grown. And maybe, in not promising Avery anything, I am promising him what he fears most. That the choices I will make over the next three months will only bring me further from his skin. "I might not have service in the woods."

"Letters? Smoke Signals?" he babbles. I want to tell him that he doesn't even make that much of an effort to communicate with me while

I am here. His vocabulary has been limited to three phrases lately, I've known three-year-olds that are more articulate. *Good Morning Beautiful. I'm sorry. I will get a job soon, I promise.* "Soon" is Avery's new favorite word. Some time "soon" things will get better. I'm running out of tomorrows.

"I love you," I say before closing the car door. He doesn't say it back. And maybe these are all the words I really need.

***

Step 2: Wash your hands with soap and water. Cover any wounds you may have with plaster.

***

The bar is the most Maine-est thing I have ever seen. Everything in it seems to be sticky to the touch, and I have the constant urge to wash my hands. It is a Wednesday, and I am sporting a Hooters tank top, celebrating a stranger's 21st birthday. I am cotton mouthed and gun shy from a day of camp icebreakers. There is nothing I can tell my coworkers about how I've been living. So I don't say much. The bar sells "I heart Poon" bumper stickers as well as "sweet poon tang punch". I watch the icy slush of it gyrating in a snow cone machine amidst the more well known liquor bottles. I wonder if that's what my brain looks like at this point. Buoys dangle from the ceiling, helping us navigate the sticky floor like some strange sea. Vintage school photos of people we will never meet stare at us all bifocal glasses and Farrah Fawcett hair from the walls.

The bar itself is scrawled over in desperate drunken handwriting. I sign my name while waiting for a vodka lemonade. I like the idea that someone will read this and wonder about me when I am far from this place. I have a feeling in my young and aching bones that tonight will be something worth memorializing. My name is but a thin and fragile landmark, but it's all I have.

I sit down at a too big chair at a table a little adrift from the other counselors. I pull out my phone to text Avery. "I miss you," I say even though I don't mean it. I miss lots of things. I miss attention, I miss my apartment, my cat, my life before I met him. My baby. But those are all complaints for greater gods.

A co-worker from our sister camp with a Jesus beard and a psychedelic goat shirt sits down in the chair beside me. I pretend not to see him. He's mountain hermit, take me to Woodstock baby attractive, but I am growing weary of this particular story line.

In the marrow of my bones, I recognize this man. My mother had seen him in a dream a few months back. She had called me on a Saturday morning to announce, "Liza, you are going to meet a man."

"Mama, I already have a man," I had told her, because Avery and I were still hopelessly trudging along.

"A better man," she had told me cryptically, before telling me about the dream she had, where she had seen me sitting on a beach, my hair shoulder short, sitting beside a boy with hair longer than my own and a full beard. My mother has dreams the way I have nightmares. Nothing means nothing. It is to your benefit to remember everything you see in the dark.

In this unfamiliar bar, I can already tell you at that moment exactly where me and this coworker will be in three hours. I have stopped wondering if the women in my mother's family can tell the future because of our Gypsy blood, a heritage of crystal balls and palm lines or whether we're just bored with the universe. Human beings are simple. If you lead a man to heels, he's probably going to drink.

I stare absentmindedly at the silent big screen TV across the bar, the face of it partially covered with the ridiculous buoys. There's a baseball game on. I don't even watch sports. There's an electric jukebox playing The Eagles singing about checking out any time you like. *If I play dead long enough, will he go away?*

"So where are you from?" he breaks the silence. I turn to look at him and it's all over. Then we're talking about paint fights and weed and times we almost got fired. We're talking about all the alcohol we've ever thrown up, about California hotel rooms and demon foxes coming to carry me away. We talk about teeth and God and 90's grunge. I tell him that *Love is a Dog From Hell* is my bible and he laughs with a smile that makes him look more canine than human.

We mix lemonade and cranberry vodka fifty fifty and decide that this combination is right. We shoot shots of Jack Daniels, and he picks on me for sipping mine.

"Please don't puke," the bartender, a rural middle aged man that was not expecting an influx of twenty-one year olds, reminds us. The boy mocks me by imitating my facial expressions, and I can no longer tell if my sudden urge to kiss him is out of fondness or if it is simply a new and warped brand of narcissism. I am laughing so long and hard that my face hurts. The boy has not hung around long enough to find this habit annoying. He has not realized yet that it is a nervous tick and little else, so he laughs too.

"Mr. Jones" by Counting Crows plays on the jukebox. "This is my song," he tells me. "I am Mr. Jones. Levi Jones"

I sling back another shot of Jack and sing along in a voice that is all whiskey-tinged lullaby.

Mr. Jones and me tell each other fairy tales.

***

Step 3: Trace the tattoo design, ideally with a tattoo stencil. If you must use a household pen, be sure not to use the same pen across different persons.

***

There are broken clamshells gnawing their way into my back and I don't mind. I wonder absentmindedly if their shapes will still be stenciled there in the morning, proof of everywhere I've been this night. Levi and I lie on the camp beach staring up at the sky because we do not know where else to go. He is only here for training, has no cabin of his own. I have a prudish and sober roommate snoring in the bed next to mine. We have run down to the beach, the very edge of the camp property, the farthest we can stray from everyone else. We are two city kids telling each other how beautiful the Maine stars are in identical words, as if we both can't see it for ourselves, as if words could ever really capture something that is as beyond us as this.

"You are beautiful," he tells me in the same tone of voice he uses to talk about the sky. Avery has worn this word down to it's bones, but it sounds different on Levi's tongue. This is why I love strangers. They haven't figured out yet that unlike the sky, I am finite.

I am all vodka breath and sun-bitten thighs. A bug bite on my eyelid. And still he says beautiful. My hair is shorter than his, shorn a shoulder cut of sharpness from the past winter when I decided I wanted to disappear, fade away into a dull smallness so that no one would notice me at all. I ask myself if I am glad now, that I made it, so that seaglass and starlight could cut me up like ribbons. So that I could hear him call this car wreck of a body beautiful.

I shake my head against his shoulder. I am being overly sentimental. This night is just a brief recess from the normal chain gang trudge of awful. I learned long ago that these moments are over while they are happening, but it's still the only thing that I can find worth living for.

I kiss him with my eyes closed, and I see galaxies that rival the ones above our heads. It's dark enough that I could pretend he is Avery. I don't.

***

Step 4: Slight improvements in stenciling might make the difference between mistakes and tattoos you're willing to show off.

***

There's an early morning breeze coming in off the ocean. The fog is rolling in like ghosts. I am walking alone from my cabin to the dining hall, staring off into the low tide mud as if it could tell me whether last night was a mistake or a sign. Gooseflesh coils up my arms like a forest fire. I walk into the dining hall at seven a.m., red eyed, black coffee awful. I'm wearing a tasseled crop top, bleached booty shorts. My shoulder length hair is done up some kind of backwoods beauty queen. Discount mascara is painted over my infected eye. A mosquito bit me on my eyelid yesterday. The man from the night before told me that it's because the insect thought my eyes were pretty too. He told me some things were too beautiful to resist. I'm more sunburnt than tan, my face looks like I'm always anime blushing, so when I walk in and the entire dining hall goes silent, none of the other counselors can see the blood rushing to my face. They stare anyways.

I pretend not to notice and go in search of a stained and chipped coffee cup. I rip open a hot chocolate packet with my teeth, as pornographically as I can manage, to give their intruding eyes a show. I pour sugar like cocaine snow and squeeze the last drop out of the coffee dispenser. I hum a love song that I stopped believing in long ago and swing my hips when I walk like Amy Winehouse.

Whispers stir around me as swift as the ocean breeze. It sounds like home. I no longer have to introduce myself. I no longer have to fumble over ice breakers. They know exactly who I am now. I'm the girl that had sex on the camp beach with a virtual stranger. I'm the girl that carried her bedding across camp this morning before the sun even came up. *But she's so quiet,* they will say. *There's no way.*

I sit next to Tina, an art student with a pixie cut and a fantastic ass. With my coffee clenched in my hungover fist, I can trace every vein in my hand, the roadmap of my blood swollen from dehydration. I pick at my pink nail polish, a shade somewhere between stripper lip gloss and Lolita bubble gum, nervously until flecks of it swirl in my pancake syrup like Birthday cake sprinkles. I eat them anyway.

"So how are you doing this morning, Liza?" Tina asks me with a familiarity we have never shared.

"Good," I chirp, and little else. Last night is not something I want to cheapen by talking about it. It's between me, a Jesus looking dude, the tide and the stars. Until I talk about it, it belongs only to us. I want to keep this safe. But it is a small camp, a small town.

My guy walks in and a half-hearted, half -joking din of applause sprinkles over the dining hall. He sits across from me, smiles a grin that looks more lupine than human. I'm reminded of the Nirvana tattoo I spotted on his right ass cheek this morning. I've always had a thing for people who don't take themselves too seriously. I've always known how to recognize salvation when I see it, and man The Killers were wrong; he looks everything like Jesus.

We eat pancakes that somebody else has made. He laughs at my stories: drunken fumblings of a lost girl who only wanted respect but made the mistake of searching for love instead. I steal glances of him over my coffee mug. I think about what Johnny Cash's idea of heaven was, having coffee with her in the morning.

"Am I your heaven?" I want to ask him. But heaven is for the dead, and we, we are just beginning.

***

Step 5: Some recommend testing the stick and poke needle in the skin without ink. This is done to see if the person being tattooed can handle the pain.

***

Levi and I are watching a girl on the precipice of a 70 ft cliff. The ledge she's standing on is some kind of Pocahontas landscape tall, looking down its nose at the black water quarry below. She'll live if she jumps; we've all been there before. The water just feels like knives when you break the surface. Your nostrils feel drug habit sore, your eyelids fling back against your will. Your limbs and bathing suit are strewn haphazardly. But you live.

The girl keeps running right up to the edge and then retreating back. Her sage green bathing suit keeps bunching up around her crotch. Her face is scrunched up in stubbornness with indecision.

"She won't jump," I tell Levi, who's holding me in the black water, like a damsel in distress. He's trying to keep me warm, trying to keep my fingers from turning as black as my bikini top. I haven't figured out how to explain to him yet that I was born cold, nothing he can ever do will thaw that.

"You don't think she will?" he asks, mockingly, challengingly "I bet she will."

The girl's stoner friends are calling to her from across the quarry, jeering and gesturing their half drunk beer cans toward her shaking legs.

"Pussy!

Get your ass in the water!"

She's shaking her head at them, "I can't!"

The friends catcall back from their perch among the graffiti spattered rocks, boulders screaming slogans like "Smoke weed every day." A spray painted Casper looking ghost stares out from where it is sprawled across the rock wall with a speech bubble balanced on his shoulder proclaiming that he is getting better. A car wreck gazes up from the bottom of the quarry, with shattered windows glittering up like broken teeth, chandelier eyes. The driver of this vehicle is long dead and no one remembers or cares how the car got there. It sits there, bearing witness, silent as a scream at the bottom of a swimming pool to all our bravery and all our stupidity.

And I'm not sure which I am right now, brave or stupid, being held by a man who is not my boyfriend, trying not to fall in anything resembling love, betting against all odds that I won't. He smells like lavender and patchouli, and the not quite clean tinge of quarry water. His breath smells like vanilla ice cream from the Captain Morgan he had for breakfast. He continues to try to reach for me, even though I keep pushing him away, even though, up until this point, I have refused to let him touch me in public.

The girl on the ledge shakes her head, turns and sprints head long back into the woods. She is backing out, even though it's way more difficult to extricate yourself from that height than to just let go and jump as you had wanted or planned to do in the first place.

"See, I told you she wouldn't do it," I tell Levi defiantly.

"You sure?" before he is even done asking the question, the girl bolts out of the underbrush and leaps off the edge without a second thought. She's flying and it's breathtaking, her copper hair flying behind her like some strange flag of surrender.

"I can't be right all the time," I tell him, pecking him on the nose before I swim away. Tomorrow he will go back to his own camp for the week. I will spend the days without him building up my courage to jump.

The last person I tell about our break up is Avery. On the way back from ice cream a week after I met Levi, in the camp van, I announce it to the entire car full of counselors. "We broke up," the lie slips through my lips as easily as my peppermint stick ice cream. But is it really a lie if it is just not true, yet? I'm breaking the news to myself gradually to see if I can handle the full impact of the clean break. I'm not sure I'm strong enough yet.

I tell everyone that we're over. I tell them that I've seen Avery's sins and denied him penitence. He is no longer welcome in my garden of Eden. I can no longer promise him my heaven. But it's all a lie, a crystal and frosting facade that shatters over my head like a stage prop in my tent that night when he texts me at 11pm. This is Avery's afternoon.

I am trying to sleep, but outside my tent, rain is ricocheting off of empty camping bowls planted amongst the mud and the dead grass. Pots and pans are turning to rust around the campfire circle because I was too lazy, was too busy, always too preoccupied with my life to do my actual fucking job.

Rain is coming down in sheets. Clean sheets, like baby blankets, nothing like the sleeping bag I've been sleeping in lately that smells everything like love but nothing like my boyfriend. There is rainwater rising up through the floor of my tent, soaking into the foot of my sleeping bag. I smile, in spite of the mildew sprouting in my bedding. The drought is over, heat lightning flashes against the canvas walls. Somewhere across the harbor, thunder groans in contentment. Rain is falling now, things will grow, and what is no longer needed will be washed away with the morning's tide.

"I am sorry beautiful," Avery's text begins. I roll my eyes. This is all he ever tells me.

"It's ok, but I'm trying to sleep," I reply. *I do not have time for you right now, love,* I want to say. I call him "love" still, even though I stopped loving him long before he started apologizing. My phone is still warm from Levi's good night text fifteen minutes ago. Levi looks too much like what Mama's church taught me salvation was for me to ignore it. The butterflies in my stomach do not even know Avery's name anymore.

"I do not have time for you right now love, I'm just trying to get some sleep," I say. I think of Hannah and Justin, a staff couple who have been dating less than a year. They finish each other's sentences, lean on each other in public as if they are only one half of the same person. Avery and I have never had this brand of familiarity. His body is a minefield. Trying to love him is like trying to defuse a bomb while blindfolded and I'm getting tired, so tired of living in the dark.

I could never invite Avery to visit me at camp. Disaster trails him like a loyal dog. I can't say that I'm much different anymore, but at least I know I am losing my soul and, as Bukowski says, that means I still have one to lose.

I have announced his time of death before this body of our love affair was even cold. I'm getting tired, I want to say, please don't ask me to resuscitate, don't ask for CPR. It's a lost cause. We're already dead.

"I can't do this," I say instead.

***

Step 6: Fill the needle with ink and start carefully poking the skin. You should feel the needle break the surface.

***

It is midnight on a Saturday. Levi and I sit on the edge of a cliff overlooking a still sea, only stars break it's surface like a thousand paparazzi flashbulbs, bobbing like witnesses to our story and all it means. The moon is piss yellow and as large as my fist when I raise it to the sky. Where we are sitting looks like the edge of the universe. My universe stops here anyway. I want for nothing beyond this edge, with his hand in mine.

Levi traces each bone in my body as if he is an archeologist taking inventory. He compliments my patchouli and tells me that I smell like the Earth, as if this temporary union were something as natural and God given as the ground beneath our bare feet. Somebody has left a candle on the cliff. I watch the flame's desperate dance against the wind. I wonder how long it can survive this way.

We're kissing slow, fingers finding loopholes in seams. We are both sitting in a puddle and we don't care. If we're not careful, we'll both roll off the cliff, like two eagles in love. This we care about and we stumble off into the woods towards camp.

We pass the mile walk back talking about living life on our own terms. We talk about our understanding of the universe. About the dead and everything we cannot see. The air is warm and the wind is blowing some kind of witching weather. The fog is setting in and softening the world at its edges. There's a story we tell the campers about the spirit of a sailor's wife rising up from the harbor, searching and mourning for a husband lost at sea while she paced helplessly across her catwalk. She spends eternity now dragging to their doom anyone who in anyway, mannerism or form resembles her dearly departed.

I see her water-bogged fingertips in every tree branch, can feel her breath on my neck, even though I know it's just the fog, just the humidity, just the lover's bite of a mosquito at the place where my skull meets my vertebrae. I am not afraid of her though; I envy her. I envy a type of love so strong that you dedicate the eternity of your eternity seeking to reclaim anything that even mildly resembles what you used to think looked like home. I have spent my whole life looking for something like that, in every secret-hiding grin, and every midnight eye, through storming nights and unwanted sunrises. At this point, I'm beginning to believe that it's all just some legend we tell ourselves in the end to keep the ghost alive. This boy I walk with now is something, but I know he will not be this love.

"Do you believe in ghosts?" Levi asks me. His voice always sounds like he has forgotten what he is saying while he is saying it. I alternate between wanting to scream at him to be more deliberate and finding this habit dopily adorable. The woods are dark. Being half drunk, my eyes make up faces behind every tree, each branch becomes a hand reaching and menacing. I snuggle in closer to his side, as if he could protect me from all that I have seen.

"I've met enough of them to know," I say, although I do not explain that I am talking about flesh and blood men. I don't preach the gospel of phones gone silent or diverted glances. I can't find the words to explain what it's like to have a body, once so solid and concrete, slip through your fingers as if they were never there. I brush the thought away. Specters hold no relevance here.

"Do you believe in God?" he asks because it is easier to fit big questions into the dark. The light of day has no space left for deities.

"I'd like to believe that there is somebody out there who forgives you, no matter what you've done," I tell him, because this is the best answer that life has left me with. He kisses me on the forehead.

"Maybe you've got to start forgiving yourself first," he says.

We come to a stop in front of a house, the front lawn and gates alight with fireflies, their bodies blinking like God's eyes in the black. These houses belong to people wealthier than we could ever dream of becoming. These dreams are somebody else's private property. Tonight I don't care. I run out onto the field, pulling Levi along behind me. We run, spin in circles like children until the world fades away around us. Until we are head over heels dizzy, laughing like maniacs in the dark. Until the grass beneath our feet squishes into mud, until fireflies light up our shirt fronts as though we are each colliding galaxies awash with stars. The fireflies cling to his beard, winking like Christmas lights against all this ebony. The porch lights come on, a dog barks. We bolt, laughing at the trouble we leave in our wake.

When the house is no longer visible in our rearview vision, we take things slow, as if we will have all the time in the world. Really we have two days at a time, a scattered brief commercial break in a sea of a TV static summer. He kisses me in stolen corners, cuts up his sentences to make space for our lips to meet between the words. I want nothing more than to lose my fingertips in the tangle of his hair.

We come home to a cabin that is only half-mine. My roommate vacates for the weekend, she knows better than to stay. Our conversation has drifted to a stop. I don't have much to say anymore. I want to apologize for the nightmares he will witness later, that I kick and thrash in my sleep fighting with ghosts he came too late to save me from.

"You hold a lot of your anxiety in your shoulder blades," he tells me, his hands trying to sculpt the worry out of my back. He was a masseuse in Virginia. I think about how all the ways we have learned to love each other have come from practicing on the skin of strangers. "Relax, I'm a professional."

My back only tenses like the coiling of a rattlesnake, dangerous, pretty and scared. He runs his fingers through my hair like he is trying to find a destiny there. It's a throwback to the days of fortune tellers, when the grooves of your skull said something about who you were and who you were going to be. I think he's trying to find a bump up there that feels something like his name.

The moonlit cabin is scattered with clothes that we are too busy or lazy to put in their proper place. We are some kind of Hozier song, just kissing like real people do. He traces a breast absentmindedly, sex with him is playground, not staircase. I can feel the outline of my heart against my rib cage. I wonder if this is what Avery felt when he did cocaine, and if it was, I could no longer blame him for being addicted. I am happy. But I can't stop thinking of the forgotten candle on the cliff, the flame wriggling like a worm on a hook just trying to stay alive. How long can this survive?

***

Warning: *If you hit blood, you've gone too far.*

***

An indie folk singer is crooning about a woman not knowing her man and the man not knowing his woman. He is singing that knowing too many people makes you cold. It is June, and I am freezing. This song is redundant for me, its message is already written in my blood.

Levi had driven us to this outdoor concert on a Saturday afternoon with a bottle of Jager balanced between his knees. I am used to Avery, I am used to being apathetic about my survival odds. This does not strike me as frightening as it should.

I am drinking straight whiskey from a Powerade bottle, praying that the security guard doing laps around the field outside L.L. Bean doesn't notice. My man is beautiful shoulder length hair and a smile that is eviler than any bone in his body. He cried in my bed that morning, and I called this honesty. He tells me drunken stories of his past, and I call this a mirror.

"What are your plans for this whole thing?" Mattie, my counselor friend, a girl with curves in all the right places and goldfish eyes, asks me on our way to the bathroom. I let go of a stolen balloon and watch it's baby blue float into a matching sky.

"I like what's going on, but that's about all I can let myself think about so far," I say, but I'm wishing on this sacrificed balloon that maybe I'll get to keep this one, but I know better by now.

While Mattie is in the bathroom, I take my bra off under my shirt in the L.L. Bean lobby and drape it around the neck of mannequin. My parents used to bring me here on long car trips. I have half-molded memories of my little brother standing ankle deep in the indoor fish pond, of my mother shoving me into snow suits in summer because that's the only time we could afford them.

Now I'm crossfaded, talking myself out of a pencil dive over the railing into the indoor waterfall. Mattie emerges from the bathroom. I'm giving her advice on how to talk to boys even though I've never really been that good at talking to anybody. We're popping marijuana gummy bears like they're just candy. Levi tells me that they have an opiate effect because they break down in your stomach, not your lungs. It's something deeper than breathing.

I just think they make me tired. They leave my mouth wreaking of skunks and strawberries, but Levi tells me I taste better this way. I accept this. My boys have always liked me better confused.

***

Step 8: Once your stick and poke tattoo is complete, clean it one last time with rubbing alcohol and apply a bandage on it.

***

It is a Wednesday night and Olly, a skeletal and twitchy twenty-year-old that I consider to be my little brother, drops a grocery bag of his shorn hair in the front seat of my car. We are driving to Augusta on our night off. Olly hands me the shredded remains of one of my father's business sweatshirts. "Sorry," he says. I want to tell Olly that it doesn't matter, that I have already ruined everything of importance that has ever bore my father's name. I want to tell him that between the sweatshirt and his skull, that he looks like he spent the day having a fist fight with a woodchipper. Instead, I run my calloused and chipped fingers through his self-shorn scalp and say "you're a beautiful mess," as if this was something new to him.

"People shave their heads as a sign of autonomy," Olly tells me, as if my chin chopped blondness isn't already proof of this. I am old enough to know that only people who have lost all control of their lives get their hair cut in any extreme. I want to ask him what he's grieving for, besides his inability to get his head out of his own ass. But I bite my tongue because I love him like a brother and other people's lives are always more easily solved than my own.

We are going to get India ink for stick and poke tattoos. I haven't defiled the temple of my body with anything in about three weeks, and I'm starting to get antsy. My walls are beginning to feel too holy. I have a sudden urge to scrawl my name in shit across the alabaster, metaphorically, of course. I have not heard from Levi in two weeks. His name has become just another ghost, another knot in my back. And I can't even pretend to be surprised. I refuse to be hurt about this. I wrap my heart in a bandage and ignore it.

Augusta is haunted. If we take a wrong turn on the rotary I can show Olly the now abandoned trap house that my dead child was conceived in. We go to Barnes and Noble. I remember wandering the stacks, too broke to buy anything, waiting for Avery to get out of work. If we go down this road a little further we will hit the bar that momentarily, for a night, at least, I fell in love with Katrina. There's a nail salon I went to religiously every other weekend last fall, as if it were a church. As if acetone were holy water, as if I could anoint myself sacred if my nails matched Avery's cocaine nose bleeds. There's the emergency room that Ben went to after putting his hand through a TV. The same emergency room Tyler went to after breaking his foot on the carpet from shadow boxing in a haunted house.

I'm talking a mile a minute, trying to explain to Olly what I'm flashing back to. My words aren't the right size to cover the way we lived.

You could only understand if you were there. Even those of us who bore witness were befuddled now by what we saw, confused by the things we had done. I don't even know how to talk about it anymore.

"I guess I just miss who Avery was when I first met him," I settle on. "But I guess that's just how nostalgia works."

Olly tells me that we're making memories while we're buying 99 cent energy drinks and hypodermic needles. He tells me that he wrote a poem about what I told him about the firefly house, a poem about me. He reads it to me from his moleskin journal while I drive, "beware the firefly girl, for the fields she runs in are wider than your dreams." I thank him. I want nothing more than to live up to Olly's opinion of me. But his words fall like a cross, an unjust weight on my shoulders. Sometimes I do not want to be poetic. I just want to be human.

We're singing along to Kendrick Lamar rapping about loyalty, about wanting someone to trust you more than you want them to love you. And maybe love and trust mean the same thing. Or maybe both those words really mean nothing at all.

***

Step 9: Know that all your equipment that was on your working area or in contact with the tattoo should be considered to be medical waste.

***

When Olly and I get back from Augusta, it is 10 p.m. I am sitting on the floor of the staff lounge, burning a sewing needle with a lighter. I am trying to recall the shape of my skull so that I can print it on my ankle. I focus on the task at hand and try to banish the ghosts that lurk around each mismatched and ripped recliner chair in this room. I try to forget that Matt and I once slept on this floor, on stolen pillows and expiration dated promises. I try to forget being trapped on the blue couch by Levi's sleeping body while *Ren and Stimpy* played on the static ridden TV in the corner. A girl like me is not supposed to remember where she has left her body. But I remember the swirls of every fingerprint, every first name. I just want something in my life that I feel ok about remembering.

"Gotta make sure your needle's sterilized," Mattie jokes. She's sitting on a puke colored chair, snapchatting duck faces to her most recent fling, a man with a beard and a beer gut. I marvel, sometimes, at how beautiful girls can get so torn up about guys we can't even call handsome. But I am not one to judge, I lost that right three one-night-stands ago. Instead, I flash her an evil smile.

"Oh I always sterilize *all* of my needles," I say with a humor that only goes skin deep. I choke back memories of a single track mark dotting Avery's veins like a Christmas star the last time he held me. I'm choking back memories of eyes placid as an empty puddle and pupils quiet as a grave.

My eyes fall on a toddler sized Timberland boot orphaned on the ground by the cubbies, a straggler from the lost and found. I try not to cry, jab the needle a little harder into the skin of my ankle. I think of the foot, the leg, the boy that was once attached to this shoe. I think of dimpled, band-aid wallpapered knee caps and tiny cargo shorts riddled with grass stains. A t-shirt advertising a sports team that his father roots for. I think of a chubby, rose lipped mouth that a mother spit wiped clean that morning in his car seat before she unbuckled him for camp. I think of his puppy dogged eyes tracing an incomprehensible and fading license plate as it tumbles down the driveway. "She'll be back," we told him. You're one of the lucky ones. She loves you. I could not say the same to my daughter. And six months post-mortem, I'm left wondering why I'm still trying to, why everything baby sized still makes me want to die.

The other counselors in the lounge are taking the rice purity test online. The rules of the test are simple: the lower the score, the more corrupted you are. My score was a 7. I took it the other day on Olly's phone at a camper's request. I bumped up the number to 17 when I said it out loud because some truths were never meant for the light.

All around me my coworkers are calling out numbers;

"75"

"56"

The lowest stops at "32". Sometimes I am too tired to speak.

It's 10:30, and I am still poking myself with a bundle of thread and a sewing needle. I should be sleeping to collect energy for tomorrow, another stressful day of forced human interaction. But I am adding layer after layer of ink still until my skin blooms black with excess. I wipe away the extra and the paper towel comes away all midnight and alcohol. And I baptize this mess my new blood, and it is truer than anything else that has ever flowed through my veins.

I have alcohol for my ankle and alcohol in a cranberry juice jug. Tequila and vodka that's helping me forget the pinpricks of pain that I'm stabbing into my ankle and the ones that Mr. Jones is poking into my heart with his silence.

"Are you mad now that you broke up with your boyfriend for him?" Mattie asks me, because I have not spoken to anyone about Levi's absence. I am not my mother, I do not speak of the dead. But I have to correct this. I will not let my story be told for me.

"I didn't break up with Avery for Levi," I say. "I did that for me."

My tattoo is finished. I have carved a death's head into my ankle. The first tattoo I have ever done with my own hands. I can't even tell you what it means, but I know it is mine. Most of my life had been defined by the marks that men had left on me. And now I was making my own.

"It suits you," Mattie says. I look at this angry, skinless smile staring back at me from my foot. A memorial to everything that has ever died in me, a herald for what has yet to be reborn from these young and tired bones. I laugh to myself and wonder where she sees the resemblance.

Acknowledgements

Thank you to those who could not love me and those who tried their damnedest, you have made me who I am. I would like to thank Jeffrey Thomson, for believing in me at a time when I couldn't even believe in myself, this book would not exist without you. Thank you to my friend and fellow writer, Olivia Cyr, for helping me to revise this book in its early stages, all writers need a community and you have been mine. Thank you to my fifth grade writing teacher, Mrs. Dubois for giving me my first writer's notebook. Thank you to my AP comp teacher, Ms. Schmidt for helping me compile my first writing portfolio, without you I would have never pursued a major in creative writing. I would like to thank my parents for always supporting my writing, even when the subject matter is not exactly their cup of tea. I would like to thank the people at Running Wild Press, specifically Lisa and Rebecca, for all their help in making this book possible. And lastly, I would like to thank my husband for always believing in me and for being the unwritten happily ever after to this story.

About the Author

Aliza Dube was raised in Deep River, CT. She graduated from the University of Maine at Farmington in 2018 with a BFA in Creative Writing and a BS in Elementary Education. Shortly after this book ends, Aliza met her husband. They now live in Eastern Kansas with their black cat and their infant son. This is Aliza's first book.

Past Titles

Running Wild Stories Anthology, Volume 1
Running Wild Anthology of Novellas, Volume 1
Jersey Diner by Lisa Diane Kastner
Magic Forgotten by Jack Hillman
The Kidnapped by Dwight L. Wilson
Running Wild Stories Anthology, Volume 2
Running Wild Novella Anthology, Volume 2, Part 1 & 2
Running Wild Novella Anthology, Volume 3, Books 1, 2, 3
Running Wild Stories Anthology, Volume 3
Running Wild's Best of 2017, AWP Special Edition
Running Wild's Best of 2018
Build Your Music Career From Scratch, Second Edition by Andrae Alexander
Writers Resist: Anthology 2018 with featured editors Sara Marchant and Kit-Bacon Gressitt
Magic Forbidden by Jack Hillman
Frontal Matter: Glue Gone Wild by Suzanne Samples
Mickey: The Giveaway Boy by Robert M. Shafer
Dark Corners by Reuben "Tihi" Hayslett
The Resistors by Dwight L. Wilson
Legendary by Amelia Kibbie
Christine, Released by E. Burke

Upcoming Titles

Running Wild Anthology of Stories, Volume 4
Running Wild Novella Anthology, Volume 4
Open My Eyes by T. E. Hahn
Recon: The Anthology by Ben White
Sodom & Gomorrah on a Saturday Night by Christa Miller
Turing's Graveyard by Terence Hawkins
Running Wild Press, Best of 2019
The Faith Machine by Tone Milazzo
Tough Love at Mystic Bay by Elizabeth Sowden
Suicide Forest by Sarah Sleeper
Magpie's Return by Curtis Smith

Running Wild Press publishes stories that cross genres with great stories and writing. Our team consists of:

Lisa Diane Kastner, Founder and Executive Editor
Barbara Lockwood, Editor
Cecile Sarruf, Editor
Peter Wright, Editor
Rebecca Dimyan, Editor
Benjamin White, Editor
Andrew DiPrinzio, Editor
Amrita Raman, Operations Manager
Lisa Montagne, Director of Education

Learn more about us and our stories at www.runningwildpress.com

Loved this story and want more? Follow us at
www.runningwildpress.com, www.facebook/runningwildpress, on
Twitter @lisadkastner @RunWildBooks

CPSIA information can be obtained
at www.ICGtesting.com
Printed in the USA
JSHW020015280421
14042JS00005B/137